Edexcel GCSE (9–1)
Combined Science

Mark Levesley Penny Johnson Sue Kearsey Iain Brand Nigel Saunders John Ling Steve Gray

Term 1

Vienna

ALWAYS LEARNING

PEARSON

Contents

Teaching and learning

The **topic reference** tells you which part of the course you are in. 'CP2b' means, 'Combined Science, Physics, unit 2, topic b'.

The **specification reference** allows you to cross reference against the specification criteria so you know which parts you are covering.

If you see an **H** icon that means that content will be assessed on the Higher Tier paper only.

CP2b Newton's First Law

Newton's First Law

Specification reference: P1.12; P1.16; P1.17

Progression questions

- What happens to the motion of an object when the forces on it are balanced?
- What can happen to the motion of an object when there is a resultant force on it?
- **H** What is centripetal force?

Sir Isaac Newton (1642–1727) worked out three 'laws' of motion that describe how forces affect the movement of objects.

Newton's First Law of motion can be written as:

- a moving object will continue to move at the same speed and direction unless an external force acts on it
- a stationary object will remain at rest unless an external force acts on it.

It is the overall resultant force that is important when you are looking at how the velocity of an object changes. Balanced forces (zero resultant force) will not change the velocity of an object. Unbalanced forces (non-zero resultant force) will change the speed and/or direction of an object.

1 **a** What is the resultant force on the human cannonball in the vertical direction when she is flying through the air?

b How will this resultant force affect her velocity?

2 Look at photo C on the previous page again. Explain how the velocity of the aeroplane will change in the:

a vertical direction

b horizontal direction.

The ice yacht in photo B is not changing speed in the vertical direction. Its weight is balanced by an upwards force from the ice.

A Human cannonballs are propelled using unbalanced forces from compressed air or springs – not using explosives!

3 A sailing boat has a forwards force of 300 N from the wind in its sails. It is travelling at a constant speed.

a What is the total force acting backwards on the sailing boat? Explain your answer.

b The ice yacht in photo B has the same force from its sails. Explain why its velocity will be increasing.

B An ice yacht can go much faster than a sailing boat in the same wind conditions.

54

H Circular motion

C This fairground ride is accelerating the people in the chairs.

An object moving in a circle has changing velocity, even though its speed remains the same. The resultant force that causes the change in direction is called the **centripetal force**, and acts towards the centre of the circle. In photo C, the centripetal force is provided by tension in the wires holding the seats. Other types of force that can make objects move in circular paths include friction and gravity.

centripetal force

D The centripetal force here is supplied by friction between the tyres and the road.

4 A satellite is in a circular orbit around the Earth. Explain how and why its velocity is continuously changing.

Exam-style question

Exam-style questions will follow on publication of the sample assessment materials by Edexcel.

Please see www.edexcel.com/gcsesci16 for more details.

Checkpoint

How confidently can you answer the questions at the top of the previous page?

Strengthen

S1 You are cycling along a flat road and your speed is increasing. Explain the resultant forces on you in the horizontal and vertical directions.

Extend

E1 Describe the forces on a human cannonball, from just before they are fired to when they land safely in a net, including how these forces affect their motion. You only need to consider forces and motion in the vertical direction.

E2 **H** Explain what a centripetal force is and describe three different kinds of force that can act as centripetal forces.

55

By the end of the topic you should be able to confidently answer the **Progression questions**. Try to answer them before you start and make a note of your answers. Think about what you know already and what more you need to learn.

Each question has been given a **Pearson Step** from 1 to 12. This tells you how difficult the question is. The higher the step the more challenging the question.

When you've worked through the main student book questions, answer the **Progression questions** again and review your own progress. Decide if you need to reinforce your own learning by answering the **Strengthen question**, or apply, analyse and evaluate your learning in new contexts by tackling the **Extend question**.

CB1 Key Biological Concepts

The bone-eating snot-flower worm (*Osedax mucofloris*) has no digestive system but still manages to feed on one of the hardest substances produced by vertebrate animals – their bones. These worms are a type of zombie worm, so-called because they have no eyes or mouth, and were discovered in the North Sea in 2005 feeding on a whale skeleton. Enzymes in the 'foot' of the worm cause the production of an acid, which attacks bone and releases lipids and proteins from inside the bone. Enzymes in bacteria on the foot of the worm then digest these large organic molecules into smaller molecules that the worms absorb (using processes such as diffusion).

In this unit you will learn about some of the central ideas in biology, including ideas about cells, microscopy, enzymes, nutrition, diffusion, osmosis and active transport.

The learning journey

Previously you will have learnt at KS3:

- how to use a microscope
- about the differences between cells from different organisms
- how some cells are specialised and adapted to their functions
- how enzymes help to digest food in the digestive system
- how substances can move by diffusion.

In this unit you will learn:

- how developments in microscopy have allowed us to find out more about the sub-cellular structures found in plant, animal and bacterial cells
- about the importance of enzymes in nutrition, growth and development
- how enzymes are affected by pH and temperature and why each enzyme only works on a certain type of molecule
- how substances are carried by diffusion, osmosis and active transport.

The 'foot' of the worm is buried in the whale bone and contains many bacteria.

CB1a Microscopes

Specification reference: B1.3; B1.4; B1.5

Progression questions

- What determines how good a microscope is at showing small details?
- What has the development of the electron microscope allowed us to do?
- What units are used for very small sizes?

A Hooke's microscope

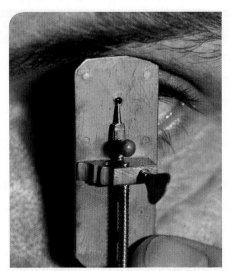

B replica of a van Leeuwenhoek microscope

The most common microscope used today contains two lenses and was invented at the end of the 16th century. Robert Hooke (1635–1703) used a microscope like this to discover cells in 1665.

Hooke's microscope had a **magnification** of about ×30 (it made things appear about 30 times bigger). A person magnified 30 times would be roughly the size of the Statue of Liberty in New York.

1 **a** A photo of a water flea says it is magnified ×50. What does this mean?

b On the photo, the flea is 5 cm long. Calculate the unmagnified length of the water flea.

To work out a microscope's magnification, you *multiply* the magnifications of its two lenses together. So, the magnification of a microscope with a ×5 **eyepiece lens** and ×10 **objective lens** is:

$$5 \times 10 = \times 50$$

2 A microscope has a ×5 eyepiece lens with ×5, ×15 and ×20 objective lenses. Calculate its three total magnifications.

Hooke's microscope was not very powerful because the glass lenses were of poor quality. Antonie van Leeuwenhoek (1632–1723) found a way of making much better lenses, although they were very small. He used these to construct microscopes with single lenses, which had magnifications of up to ×270. In 1675, he examined a drop of rainwater and was surprised to find tiny organisms, which he called 'animalcules'. Fascinated by his discovery, he searched for 'animalcules' in different places.

3 The top bacterium in photo C is 0.002 mm long in real life. At what magnification is the drawing?

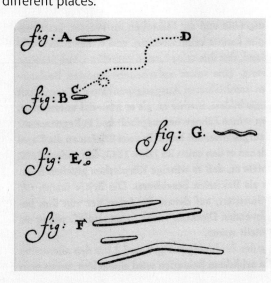

C These are van Leeuwenhoek's drawings of 'animalcules' found in scrapings from his teeth. We call them bacteria.

Did you know?

Van Leeuwenhoek examined his semen and discovered sperm cells.

The detail obtained by a microscope also depends on its **resolution**. This is the smallest distance between two points that can still be seen as two points. Van Leeuwenhoek's best microscopes had a resolution of 0.0014 mm. Two points that were 0.0014 mm or further apart could be seen as two points, but two points closer together than this appeared as a single point.

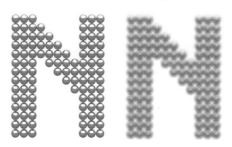

D These images of tiny beads have the same magnification but different resolutions.

 4   Hooke's microscope had a resolution of about 0.002 mm. What does this mean?

With the development of **stains** for specimens, and better lenses and light sources, today's best light microscopes magnify up to ×1500 with resolutions down to about 0.0001 mm.

The electron microscope was invented in the 1930s. Instead of light, beams of electrons pass through a specimen to build up an image. These microscopes can magnify up to ×2 000 000, with resolutions down to 0.0000002 mm. They allow us to see cells with great detail and clarity.

 5   Explain why electron microscope images show more detail than light microscopes.

SI units

The measurements on these pages are in millimetres. Adding the 'milli' prefix to a unit divides it by 1000. One metre (m) contains 1000 millimetres (mm). There are other prefixes that often make numbers easier to understand.

Table E

Prefix	Effect on unit	Example
milli-	÷ 1000	millimetres (mm)
micro-	÷ 1 000 000	micrometres (μm)
nano-	÷ 1 000 000 000	nanometres (nm)
pico-	÷ 1 000 000 000 000	picometres (pm)

× 1000   × 1000   × 1000   ÷ 1000   ÷ 1000   ÷ 1000

 6   Give the highest resolution of electron microscopes in micro-, nano- and picometres.

Exam-style question

Exam-style questions will follow on publication of the sample assessment materials by Edexcel.

Please see www.edexcel.com/gcsesci16 for more details.

Checkpoint

How confidently can you answer the questions at the top of the previous page?

Strengthen

S1 Compare today's light microscopes with Hooke's.

Extend

E1 Diatoms are algae, 20–120 μm in length and with 1 μm diameter 'pores' in their outer coats. Van Leeuwenhoek described diatom shapes but not their pores. Explain why.

Progression questions

- How are animal cells different to plant cells?
- What do the sub-cellular structures in eukaryotic cells do?
- How can we estimate the sizes of cells and their parts?

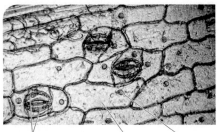

two guard cells (form a stoma in the surface of a leaf)   leaf surface cell   nucleus

A This micrograph ('microscope picture') was taken using Brown's original microscope, of the same cells in which he discovered nuclei (magnification ×67).

As microscopes improved, scientists saw more details inside cells. In 1828, Robert Brown (1773–1858) examined cells from the surface of a leaf and noticed that each cell contained a small, round blob. He called this the **nucleus** (meaning 'inner part' in Latin).

⑤ 1 Photo A is at a magnification of 67. State what this means.

Brown wrote a **scientific paper** about his discovery. Matthias Schleiden (1804–1881) read the paper and thought that the nucleus must be the most important part of a plant cell. He mentioned this idea to Theodor Schwann (1810–1882), who then wondered if he could find cells with nuclei in animals. He did. And so the idea of cells being the basic building blocks of all life was born.

A cell with a nucleus is described as **eukaryotic**. We have now discovered many other sub-cellular ('smaller than a cell') structures in eukaryotic cells and worked out what they do.

The **cell membrane** is like a very thin bag. It controls what enters and leaves, and separates one cell from another.

The **cytoplasm** contains a watery jelly and is where most of the cell's activities occur.

One of these blobs is a **mitochondrion** (see photo C). Mitochondria are jelly-bean shaped structures in which **aerobic respiration** occurs. Mitochondria are very difficult to see with a light microscope.

The **nucleus** controls the cell and its activities. Inside it are **chromosomes**, which contain **DNA**. It is especially large in white blood cells.

red blood cell

The cytoplasm also contains tiny round structures called **ribosomes**. These make new proteins for a cell. It is impossible to see them with a light microscope.

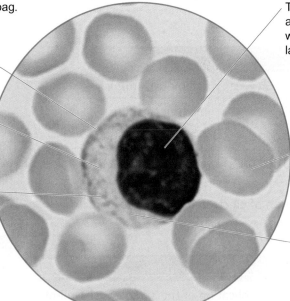

⑤ 2 Draw a table to show the parts of an animal cell and the function of each part.

B The labelled central cell is a human white blood cell, which has been stained to make its features show up clearly (magnification ×1900).

⑥ 3 Estimate the diameter of the labelled red blood cell in photo B. Show your working.

The circular area you see in a light microscope is the **field of view**. If we know its diameter, we can estimate sizes. The diameter of the field of view in photo B is 36 μm. We can imagine that three white blood cells will roughly fit across the field of view. So the cell's diameter is about $\frac{36}{3} = 12$ μm.

Electron micrographs

Photo C shows many parts inside a white blood cell that you cannot see with a light microscope. However, you still cannot see ribosomes because they are only about 25 nm in diameter.

 4 a Look at photo C. What part has been coloured purple?

 b Use the magnification to estimate the width of the cell.

 5 State the diameter of a ribosome in micrometres.

Scale bars are often shown on micrographs and these are also used to estimate sizes. The scale bar on photo C shows how long 4 μm is at this magnification. About three of these bars could fit across the cell at its widest point; the cell is about 3 × 4 = 12 μm wide.

Plant cells may have some additional structures compared with animal cells, as shown in diagram D.

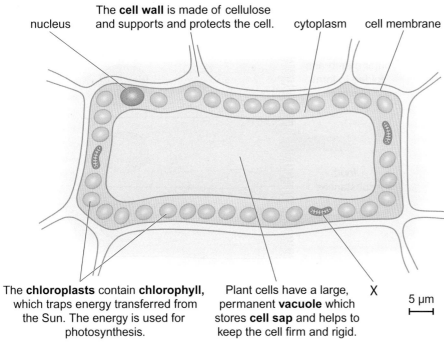

The **cell wall** is made of cellulose and supports and protects the cell.

nucleus

cytoplasm

cell membrane

The **chloroplasts** contain **chlorophyll,** which traps energy transferred from the Sun. The energy is used for photosynthesis.

Plant cells have a large, permanent **vacuole** which stores **cell sap** and helps to keep the cell firm and rigid.

X

5 μm

D a cell from inside a plant leaf

 7 Look at diagram D. What is part X?

 8 Cells on leaf *surfaces* contain vacuoles and carry out aerobic respiration but are not green. Suggest what part they lack. Explain your reasoning.

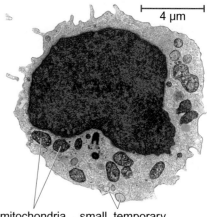

4 μm

mitochondria   small, temporary vacuoles

C electron micrograph of a white blood cell (magnification ×3800)

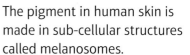

Did you know?

The pigment in human skin is made in sub-cellular structures called melanosomes.

6 Use the scale bar on photo C to estimate the:

 a width of the nucleus at its widest point

 b length of the longest mitochondrion (coloured red).

Checkpoint

How confidently can you answer the questions at the top of the previous page?

Strengthen

S1 Draw a plant cell and label its parts, describing what each part does.

Extend

E1 An 'organelle' is a structure inside a cell with a specific function. Compare the organelles found in plant and animal cells.

Exam-style question

Exam-style questions will follow on publication of the sample assessment materials by Edexcel.

Please see www.edexcel.com/gcsesci16 for more details.

CB1c Specialised cells

Specification reference: B1.2; B1.4; B1.6

Progression questions

- How are some specialised cells adapted to their functions?
- What is the function of a gamete?
- What is the function of cilia?

Did you know?

Human nerve cells (neurones) carry information very quickly. Many are adapted by being extremely long, with some reaching lengths of about 1.4 m.

Specialised cells have a specific function (job). There are about 200 different types of specialised cells in humans. All human cells have the same basic design, but their sizes, shapes and sub-cellular structures can be different so that specialised cells are **adapted** to their functions.

5 **1** List three specialised human cells and state their functions.

Specialised cells for digestion

The cells that line the small intestine absorb small food molecules produced by **digestion**. They are adapted by having membranes with many tiny folds (called **microvilli**). These **adaptations** increase the surface area of the cell. The more area for molecules to be absorbed, the faster absorption happens.

5 **2** **a** Draw a small intestine cell and label its parts.

7 **b** These cells are 20 μm long. Add a 10 μm scale bar to your drawing.

6 **c** Explain why a cell with microvilli absorbs substances more quickly than one without.

7 **3** Cells called hepatocytes make a lot of a substance called serum albumin. These cells contain many ribosomes. Suggest what type of substance serum albumin is. Explain your reasoning.

8 **4** Nerve cells require a lot of energy. Suggest the adaptation that allows them to get enough energy.

6 **5** **a** State whether a sperm cell is haploid or diploid.

7 **b** Explain why it needs to be like this.

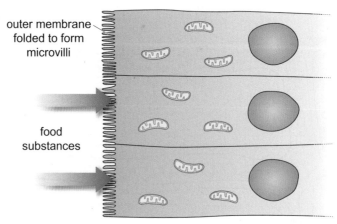

outer membrane folded to form microvilli

food substances

A small intestine cells

Cells in an organ called the pancreas make **enzymes** needed to digest certain foods in the small intestine. The enzymes are proteins and so these cells are adapted by having a lot of ribosomes.

The wall of the small intestine has muscles to squeeze food along. The muscle cells require a lot of energy and are adapted by having many mitochondria.

Specialised cells for reproduction

During sexual reproduction, two specialised cells (**gametes**) fuse to create a cell that develops into an **embryo**. Human gametes are the **egg cell** and the **sperm cell**.

Most human cell nuclei contain two copies of the 23 different types of chromosome. Gametes contain just *one* copy of each. This means that the cell produced by **fertilisation** has two copies. Cells with two sets of chromosomes are **diploid** and those with one copy of each chromosome are **haploid**.

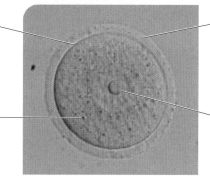

The cell membrane fuses with the sperm cell membrane. After fertilisation, the cell membrane becomes hard to stop other sperm cells entering.

The jelly coat protects the egg cell. It also hardens after fertilisation, to ensure that only one sperm cell enters the egg cell.

The cytoplasm is packed with nutrients, to supply the fertilised egg cell with energy and raw materials for the growth and development of the embryo.

haploid nucleus

B adaptations of a human female gamete

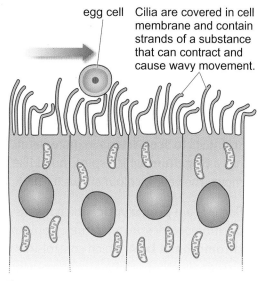

streamlined shape

The tip of the head contains a small vacuole called the **acrosome.** It contains enzymes that break down the substances in the egg cell's jelly coat. This allows the sperm cell to burrow inside.

nucleus

A large number of mitochondria are arranged in a spiral around the top of the tail, to release lots of energy to power the tail.

The tail waves from side to side, allowing the sperm cell to swim.

cell surface membrane

10 µm

C adaptations of a human male gamete

Fertilisation occurs in the **oviducts** of the female reproductive system. Cells in the lining of the oviduct transport egg cells (or the developing embryos after fertilisation) towards the uterus. The oviduct cells are adapted for this function by having hair-like **cilia**. These are like short sperm cell tails and wave from side to side to sweep substances along. Cells that line structures in the body are called **epithelial cells**, and epithelial cells with cilia are called **ciliated epithelial cells**.

egg cell

Cilia are covered in cell membrane and contain strands of a substance that can contract and cause wavy movement.

D adaptations of oviduct lining cells

7 Compare and contrast microvilli and cilia.

8 Explain why an egg cell does not need a tail but a sperm cell does.

6 a Make a drawing of a human egg cell and label its parts.

b Describe how an egg cell is adapted to prevent more than one sperm cell entering.

c A human egg cell has a diameter of 0.1 mm. Calculate the magnification of your drawing.

Checkpoint

How confidently can you answer the questions at the top of the previous page?

Strengthen

S1 List the steps that occur between an egg cell entering an oviduct and it becoming an embryo, and explain how adaptations of specialised cells help each step.

Extend

E1 Explain how both human gametes are adapted to ensure that the cell produced by fertilisation can grow and develop.

Exam-style question

Exam-style questions will follow on publication of the sample assessment materials by Edexcel.

Please see www.edexcel.com/gcsesci16 for more details.

CB1d Inside bacteria

Specification reference: B1.1; B1.5

Progression questions

- What are the functions of the sub-cellular structures in bacteria?
- What are the differences between prokaryotic and eukaryotic cells?
- How do we change numbers to and from standard form?

Bacteria are difficult to see with light microscopes because they are very small and mostly colourless. Stains are often used to make them show up.

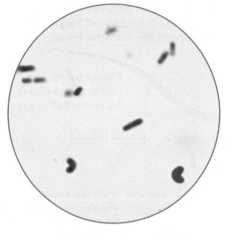

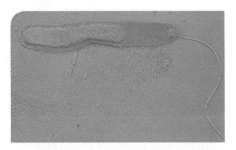

 1 a Estimate the size of one bacterium in photo A. Explain your reasoning.

 b The length of the bacterium in photo B is 3.8 cm (without its tail). Calculate its size in real life. Show all your working.

A light micrograph of *Vibrio cholerae* bacteria stained with safranin (field of view = 20 μm)

B electron micrograph of *Vibrio cholerae* bacterium, with colours added by a computer (magnification ×12 600)

The extra magnification and resolution of an electron microscope allow scientists to see bacteria in more detail. Photo B shows that this bacterium has a **flagellum**, which spins round like a propeller so the bacterium can move. The yellow colour shows its **DNA**.

Bacteria are **prokaryotic**, which means that their cells do not have nuclei or chromosomes. Instead, the cytoplasm contains one large loop of **chromosomal DNA**, which controls most of the cell's activities. There are also smaller loops of DNA, called **plasmids** (shown in photo C). **Plasmid DNA** controls a few of the cell's activities. Prokaryotic cells do not have mitochondria or chloroplasts.

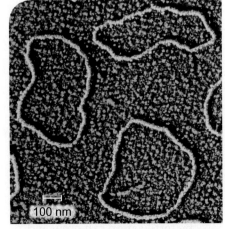

C electron micrograph of plasmids from a bacterium (magnification ×50 000)

2 a Describe the location of the plasmid in photo B.

b Give the name of the substance it is made from.

c Where is this substance mainly found in a eukaryotic cell?

3 Describe the function of a bacterium's flagellum.

Information from microscope images and other work has allowed scientists to discover more about the parts of bacterial cells and their functions, as shown in diagram D.

flagellum (is not covered in a membrane and not all bacteria have them, but some have many flagella)

plasmids   chromosomal DNA

slime coat (for protection – not all bacteria have this)

flexible cell wall (for support – not made out of cellulose)

cell membrane

cytoplasm (contains ribosomes, which are smaller than eukaryotic ribosomes)

D Different bacteria are different shapes and sizes but usually have these parts.

Standard form

A prokaryotic ribosome is 20 nm in diameter and a football is 0.22 m in diameter. It is hard to compare these sizes because they have different units.

1 m is 1 000 000 000 nm, so a football is 220 000 000 nm in diameter. The units are now the same but figures with so many zeros can be difficult to read and use. To solve this problem, we can show figures in the form of a number between 1 and 10 multiplied by a power of 10.

$$A \times 10^n$$

where A is between 1 and 10 and n is the power of 10; n is also called the **index** number. This is **standard form**. The index number tells you how many place values to move the digit.

For numbers greater than 0, count how many times you need to move the unit to the right until you form a number between 1 and 10.

Write this number as the power of 10, insert the decimal point and remove the zeros.

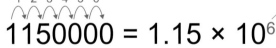

$$1150000 = 1.15 \times 10^6$$

For numbers less than 0, count how many times you need to move the unit to the left until you form a number between 1 and 10.

This becomes a negative power.

$$0.0000007 = 7 \times 10^{-8}$$

E writing numbers in standard form

Make sure you know how to input numbers in standard form on your calculator.

Exam-style question

Exam-style questions will follow on publication of the sample assessment materials by Edexcel.

Please see www.edexcel.com/gcsesci16 for more details.

 4 Draw a table to show the functions of the different parts of a bacterial cell.

 5 Estimate the diameter of one plasmid shown in photo C.

 6 Suggest why ribosomes are not shown on diagram D.

Did you know?

Your body contains more bacterial cells than human cells. Most of these are found in the digestive system.

7 Make a copy of table E from CB1a, adding another column to show in standard form the effect of adding each prefix. For example, 'milli-' divides a number by a thousand, which in standard form is the same as multiplying by 10^{-3}.

8 Write the diameters of a ribosome and a football in metres in standard form.

Checkpoint

How confidently can you answer the questions at the top of the previous page?

Strengthen

S1 Draw a bacterium and label its parts, describing what each part does.

Extend

E1 Compare eukaryotic and prokaryotic cells.

CB1e Enzymes and nutrition

Specification reference: B1.12

Progression questions

- What are enzymes made out of?
- What do enzymes do?
- Why are enzymes important for life?

Most animals get substances for energy, growth and development by digesting food inside their bodies. Bacteria, on the other hand, release digestive enzymes into their environments and then absorb digested food into their cells. Starfish use a similar trick for large items of food.

In humans, digestive enzymes turn the large molcules in our food into the smaller subunits they are made of. The digested molecules are then small enough to be absorbed by the small intenstine.

A To eat large items of food, a starfish pushes its stomach out of its mouth and into the food. The stomach surface releases enzymes to break down the food, which can then be absorbed.

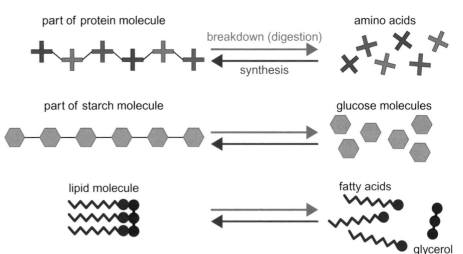

1 Which small molecules make up the following large molecules?

a carbohydrates

b proteins

c lipids

2 When you chew a piece of starchy bread for a while it starts to taste sweet. Suggest a reason for this.

3 Which monomers make up:

a proteins

b carbohydrates?

B Large molecules such as carbohydrates, proteins and lipids (fats and oils) are built from smaller molecules.

Once the small molecules are absorbed into the body, they can be used to build the larger molecules that are needed in cells and tissues. Building larger molecules from smaller subunits is known as **synthesis**. Carbohydrates and proteins are both **polymers** because they are made up of many similar small molecules, or **monomers**, joined in a chain.

The breakdown of large molecules happens incredibly slowly and only if the bonds between the smaller subunits have enough energy to break. Synthesis also happens very slowly, since the subunits rarely collide with enough force or in the right orientation to form a bond. These reactions happen much too slowly to supply all that the body needs to stay alive and be active.

Many reactions can be speeded up using a **catalyst**. In living organisms, the catalysts that speed up breakdown (e.g. digestion) and synthesis reactions are enzymes. So enzymes are **biological catalysts** that increase the rate of reactions. Enzymes are a special group of proteins that are found throughout the body. The substances that enzymes work on are called **substrates**, and the substances that are produced are called **products**.

 4 Define the term 'biological catalyst'.

 5 a Which type of smaller molecule are enzymes built from?

 b Explain your answer.

Enzyme name	Where found	Reaction catalysed
amylase	saliva and small intestine	breaking down starch to small sugars, such as maltose
catalase	most cells, but especially liver cells	breaking down hydrogen peroxide made in many cell reactions to water and oxygen
starch synthase	plant	synthesis of starch from glucose
DNA polymerase	nucleus	synthesis of DNA from its monomers

C examples of enzymes, where they are found and what they do

 6 Name the substrate of amylase, and the products of the reaction it catalyses.

 7 Give two examples of processes that are controlled by enzymes in the human body.

 8 Suggest what will happen in the cells of someone who does not make phenylalanine hydroxylase. Explain your answer.

 9 Sketch a diagram or flowchart to explain how the starfish in photo A absorbs food molecules into its body.

Exam-style question

Exam-style questions will follow on publication of the sample assessment materials by Edexcel.

Please see www.edexcel.com/gcsesci16 for more details.

Did you know?

The heel prick test takes a small amount of blood to test for several factors, including the enzyme phenylalanine hydroxylase. This enzyme catalyses the breakdown of an amino acid called phenylalanine. A few babies are born without the ability to make the enzyme, which can result in nerve and brain damage as they grow older.

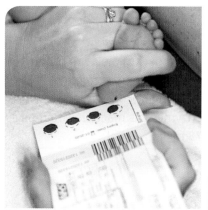

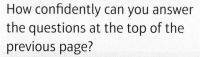

D Babies are given the heel prick test before they are a week old.

Checkpoint

How confidently can you answer the questions at the top of the previous page?

Strengthen

S1 Draw a concept map that includes all the important points on these pages. Link words to show how they are related.

Extend

E1 Many bacteria have flexible cell walls made by linking together chains of a polymer. The links are formed in reactions catalysed by an enzyme. Penicillin stops this enzyme from working. Explain how penicillin causes bacteria to be weakened.

CB1f Enzyme action

Specification reference: B1.7; B1.8

Progression questions

- What is the function of the active site of an enzyme?
- Why do enzymes only work on specific substrates?
- How are enzymes denatured?

Did you know?

There are about 3000 different enzymes in the human body, catalysing reactions that would otherwise not occur. For example, an enzyme called OMP decarboxylase helps to produce a substance used to make DNA in 18 milliseconds. Without the enzyme, this reaction would take 78 million years!

A The bombardier beetle repels attackers by releasing a very hot, foul liquid. The liquid is made by enzymes that rapidly break down substances (including hydrogen peroxide) in a reaction chamber at the end of the beetle's body.

A protein is a large three-dimensional (3D) molecule formed from a chain of amino acids. The 3D shape is caused by folding of the chain, which depends on the sequence of the amino acids in the chain. The 3D shape of enzymes is important in how they work, because within that shape is a small pocket called the **active site**.

The active site is where the substrate of the enzyme fits at the start of a reaction. Different substrates have different 3D shapes, and different enzymes have active sites of different shapes. This explains why every enzyme can only work with **specific** substrates that fit the active site.

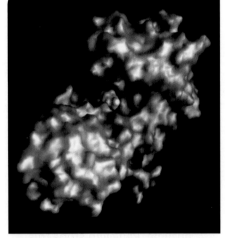

B Glucose is the substrate for the enzyme hexokinase (blue). The substrate (yellow) fits neatly within the enzyme's active site.

 1 What is the active site of an enzyme?

 2 Why is the active site a different shape in different enzymes?

 3 What is meant by 'enzyme specificity'?

One model of how enzymes work is called the **lock-and-key model**, because of how the enzyme and substrate fit together.

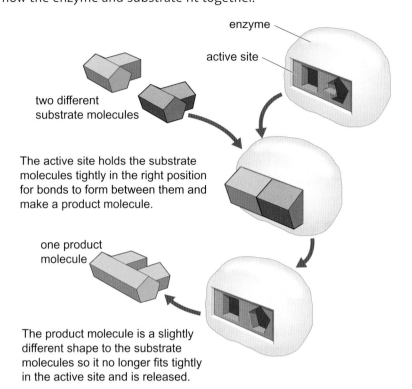

enzyme

active site

two different substrate molecules

The active site holds the substrate molecules tightly in the right position for bonds to form between them and make a product molecule.

one product molecule

The product molecule is a slightly different shape to the substrate molecules so it no longer fits tightly in the active site and is released.

C When substrate molecules are held in the right position in the active site, the bonds between them are more easily broken and formed.

Changes in pH or temperature can affect how the protein folds up, and so can affect the shape of the active site. If the shape of the active site changes too much, the substrate will no longer fit neatly in it. If the active site changes shape too much, the enzyme will no longer catalyse the reaction. We say that the enzyme has been **denatured**.

 6 Explain what denaturing of an enzyme means.

 7 Systems in humans keep our body temperatures constant. Using your knowledge of enzymes, explain why this is important.

 4 Explain why amylase does not break down proteins.

 5 Use the lock-and-key model to suggest how an amylase enzyme catalyses the breakdown of starch to small sugar molecules.

normal conditions

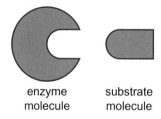

enzyme molecule   substrate molecule

extreme conditions

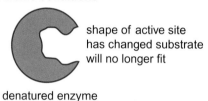

shape of active site has changed substrate will no longer fit

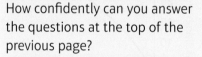

denatured enzyme

D Changes in an enzyme's environment can change the shape of the active site.

Checkpoint

How confidently can you answer the questions at the top of the previous page?

Strengthen

S1 Sketch one flowchart to show how an enzyme normally works, and another to show what happens when the enzyme is denatured.

Extend

E1 Sketch labelled diagrams to show the following:

a why enzymes have a particular shape

b why enzymes are specific to a particular substrate

c what happens when an enzyme is denatured.

Exam-style question

Exam-style questions will follow on publication of the sample assessment materials by Edexcel.

Please see www.edexcel.com/gcsesci16 for more details.

CB1g Enzyme activity

Specification reference: B1.9; B1.10; B1.11

Progression questions

- How is enzyme activity affected by temperature, pH and substrate concentration?
- How do you calculate the rate of enzyme activity?
- Why is enzyme activity affected by temperature, pH and substrate concentration?

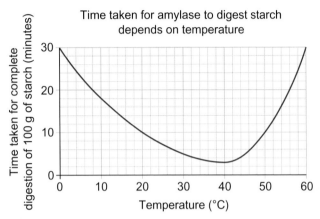

A results from experiments at different temperatures combined on to one graph

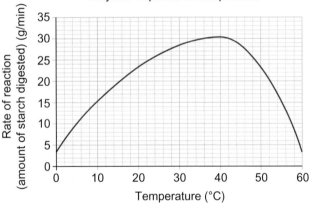

B the data in graph A shown as a rate of reaction graph

 3 a Identify the optimum temperature for the enzyme shown in graph B.

 b Explain your answer.

4 Explain why enzymes work more slowly when the temperature is:

 a below the optimum

 b above the optimum.

Enzymes are affected by the conditions in their surroundings. The results of a series of experiments that measure the time taken for an enzyme to complete the breakdown of a substrate at different temperatures can be combined to produce a graph.

 1 Use graph A to identify how long it took for the complete breakdown of starch at the following temperatures:

    a 10 °C   **b** 40 °C   **c** 50 °C.

 2 Suggest an explanation for the difference in reaction rates at 40 °C and 50 °C.

Graph A can be converted to a graph showing the rate of reaction by calculating the amount of substrate broken down or product formed in a given time. For example, graph A shows that, at 30 °C, 100 g of starch was broken down in 5 min. The mean rate of reaction was:

$$\frac{100}{5} = 20 \text{ g/min}$$

Converting the values in graph A in this way gives graph B.

Why does graph B have this shape?

- As the temperature increases, molecules move faster. Higher speeds increase the chance of substrate molecules bumping into enzyme molecules and slotting into the active site.
- However, when the temperature gets too high, the shape of the enzyme molecule starts to change. The amount of change increases as the temperature increases. So it becomes more and more difficult for a substrate molecule to fit into the active site.

The temperature at which an enzyme works fastest is called its **optimum temperature**.

Did you know?

Many human enzymes have an optimum temperature of around 37 °C.

Enzymes are now used in many processes in industry. Some industrial processes take place at high temperatures, so the search for new enzymes that have a high optimum temperature is important.

Some other factors that affect the rate of an enzyme-controlled reaction are pH and the concentration of the substrate, as shown in graphs D and E.

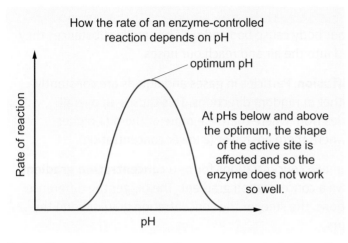

D the effect of pH on the rate of an enzyme-controlled reaction

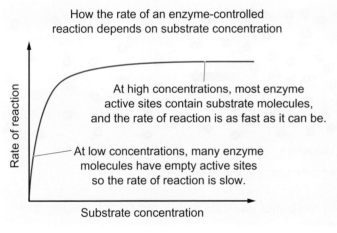

E the effect of substrate concentration on the rate of an enzyme-controlled reaction

 6 Explain the effect of substrate concentration on the rate of an enzyme-controlled reaction.

 7 The pH in the stomach is about 2, but in the small intestine it is about 6. Explain why different protease enzymes are found in the two digestive organs.

Exam-style question

Exam-style questions will follow on publication of the sample assessment materials by Edexcel.

Please see www.edexcel.com/gcsesci16 for more details.

C The bacterium *Thermus aquaticus* was discovered growing in this hotspring pool, which is at about 70 °C.

 5 a Sketch a graph to show the effect of pH on the enzyme pepsin, which has an **optimum pH** of 2.

 b Annotate your sketch to explain the shape.

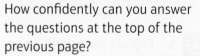

Checkpoint

How confidently can you answer the questions at the top of the previous page?

Strengthen

S1 Close the book, then sketch and annotate a graph to show how temperature affects the rate of an enzyme-controlled reaction.

Extend

E1 A manufacturer is testing several high-temperature cellulase enzymes to break down plant cell walls in plant waste used for making biofuels. Suggest how the manufacturer might carry out the test and how they would decide which is the best enzyme for this process.

CB1h Transporting substances

Specification reference: B1.15; B1.17

Progression questions

- What is the difference between diffusion and osmosis?
- How do cells move substances against a concentration gradient?
- How do you calculate a percentage change in mass?

A an experiment to assess body odour

Bacteria living on your body cause body odour. The smelly substances they produce are released into the air and reach our noses.

Smells spread by **diffusion**. Particles in gases and liquids are constantly moving past each other in random directions. This causes an overall movement of particles from where there are more of them (a higher **concentration**) to where there are fewer (a lower concentration).

A difference between two concentrations forms a **concentration gradient**. Particles diffuse *down* a concentration gradient. The bigger the difference between concentrations, the steeper the concentration gradient and the faster diffusion occurs.

The number of particles *decreases* as you go *down* a concentration gradient.

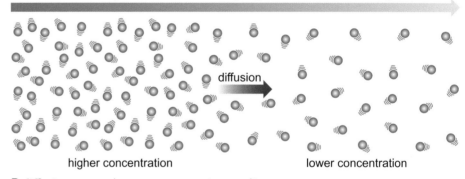

diffusion

higher concentration   lower concentration

B diffusion occurs down a concentration gradient

Diffusion allows small molecules (such as oxygen and carbon dioxide) to move into and out of cells.

1 Explain why smells spread.

2 a A dish of perfume is put at the front of a lab. Describe the perfume's concentration gradient after 5 minutes.

b Describe the overall movement of the perfume molecules.

3 Muscle cells in the leg use up oxygen but are surrounded by a fluid containing a lot of oxygen. Explain why oxygen moves into the cells.

Osmosis

A membrane that allows some molecules through and not others is **semi-permeable**.

Cell membranes are semi-permeable and trap large soluble molecules inside cells, but water molecules can diffuse through the membrane. If there are more water molecules in a certain volume on one side of the membrane than the other, there will be an overall movement of water molecules from the side where there are more water molecules (a more dilute **solute** concentration) to the side where there are fewer water molecules (a more concentrated solution of solute). This diffusion of small molecules of a **solvent**, such as water, through a semi-permeable membrane is called **osmosis**. The overall movement of solvent molecules will stop when the concentration of solutes is the same on both sides of a membrane.

4 a In diagram C, in which direction will water flow, X to Y or Y to X?

 b Explain why this flow occurs.

 5 Red blood cells contain many solute molecules. Explain why red blood cells burst if put in pure water.

Osmosis can cause tissues to gain or lose mass. To calculate the mass change:

- work out the difference between the mass of tissue at the start and at the end (start mass – final mass)
- divide this difference by the start mass
- multiply by 100.

So, percentage change in mass = $\dfrac{\text{(start mass – final mass)}}{\text{start mass}} \times 100$

A negative answer is a percentage *loss* in mass.

 6 An 8 g piece of potato is left in water for an hour. Its mass becomes 8.5 g. Calculate the percentage change in mass.

Active transport

Cells may need to transport molecules *against* a concentration gradient or transport molecules that are too big to diffuse through the cell membrane. They can do this using **active transport**.

This process is carried out by transport proteins in cell membranes. The transport proteins capture certain molecules and carry them across the cell membrane. This is an active process and so requires energy. Osmosis and diffusion are **passive** processes, so do not require an input of energy.

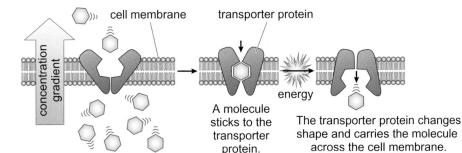

cell membrane   transporter protein

concentration gradient

energy

A molecule sticks to the transporter protein.

The transporter protein changes shape and carries the molecule across the cell membrane.

D active transport

 8 Explain how cells that carry out a lot of active transport would be adapted to their function.

Exam-style question

Exam-style questions will follow on publication of the sample assessment materials by Edexcel.

Please see www.edexcel.com/gcsesci16 for more details.

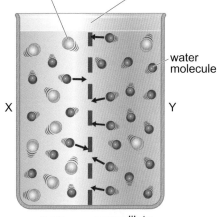

soluble molecule that is too large to pass through the membrane (e.g. sucrose)

partially permeable membrane allows molecules to pass through if they are small enough

water molecule

X   Y

more concentrated solution

more dilute solution

C In osmosis, a solvent flows from a dilute solution of a solute to a more concentrated one.

 7 Look at diagram D. Explain why active transport is needed to move the molecules.

Checkpoint

How confidently can you answer the questions at the top of the previous page?

Strengthen

S1 A small number of sugar molecules are in your small intestine. Describe how they will be absorbed into cells in the small intestine and why they need to be absorbed in this way.

Extend

E1 Sorbitol is a sweet-tasting substance that is not broken down or absorbed by the body. It is used in some sugar-free sweets. Explain why eating too many of these sweets can cause diarrhoea.

Term 1

Exam-style questions and sample student answers with expert commentary and exam tips will follow on publication of the sample assessment materials by Edexcel.

Please see www.edexcel.com/gcsesci16 for more details.

Paper 3

CC1 States of Matter /
CC2 Methods of Separating and Purifying Substances

Millions of tonnes of tiny bits of plastic are floating in the oceans, and they harm wildlife. Water currents cause the plastic to collect in certain areas. The biggest of these is the 'Great Pacific Garbage Patch' in the Pacific Ocean, which could be three times the area of the UK. At the age of 19, Dutch student Boyan Slat came up with the idea of using giant floating booms to direct the plastic pieces into a mechanism that would filter the plastic out of the water. The idea relies on two properties of the plastic – it floats and it is insoluble in water. Not everyone agrees that it will work, and think that the system would not survive in the oceans. In this unit you will learn about how materials can be separated from one another using their properties.

The learning journey

Previously you have learnt at KS3:

- how particles are arranged in solids, liquids and gases and how their energy changes with changes of state
- how mixtures differ from pure substances
- how to separate some mixtures using filtration, distillation and chromatography.

In this unit you will learn:

- how to use information to predict the state of a substance
- how the arrangement, movement and energy of particles change during changes of state
- how to use melting points to tell the difference between mixtures and pure substances
- how to identify substances using melting points and chromatography
- how different methods of separation work
- how to choose a separation method based on the properties of the substances in a mixture.

CC1a States of matter

Specification reference: C2.1; C2.2; C2.3; C2.4

Progression questions

- What are particles like in substances in the solid, liquid and gas states?
- What changes happen to particles during the different changes of state?
- How do you decide what state a substance will be in at a given temperature?

A This 'ice hotel' is made entirely from ice and snow – these are both water in the solid state.

The three **states of matter** are solid, liquid and gas. For example, water can exist in the solid state as ice, or in the familiar liquid state, or in the gas state as steam or water vapour.

The particle model

Some **particles** are large enough to see, like the dust on a computer screen. Others, like **atoms** and **molecules**, are far too small for you to see. When chemists discuss particles, they usually mean these very small particles.

The **particle model** explains state changes in a substance in terms of the arrangement, movement and energy stored in its particles.

State	Particle diagram	Arrangement of particles	Movement of particles
Gas		random far apart	fast in all directions
Liquid		random close together	move around each other
Solid		regular close together	vibrate about fixed positions

B Particles in the solid state contain the smallest amount of stored energy; particles in the gas state contain the most.

Did you know?

Science recognises 16 different types of ice, depending on the arrangement of the water molecules. A type called amorphous ice is found in space (such as on comets). A type called Ice IV is what you'll find in a kitchen freezer, here on Earth.

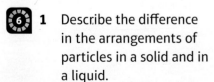 **1** Describe the difference in the arrangements of particles in a solid and in a liquid.

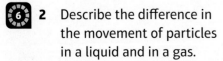 **2** Describe the difference in the movement of particles in a liquid and in a gas.

State changes

State changes are **physical changes**. They can be reversed, and the **chemical properties** of the substance do not change. This is because the particles themselves do not change – only their arrangement, movement and amount of stored energy.

 3 Describe the meaning of the terms 'sublimation' and 'deposition'.

Particles are attracted to one another by weak forces of attraction. There are many of these forces in a solid. Some of these are overcome during melting. The remaining **attractive forces** between particles in a liquid are overcome during evaporation and boiling (when a substance is evaporating as fast as it can). For this to happen, energy must be transferred from the surroundings to the particles. This is why you heat ice to melt it, and why you boil water in a kettle. Diagram D shows how the temperature changes when water in the solid state is heated until it reaches the gas state.

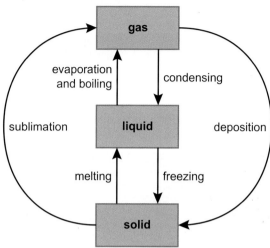

C the interconversions between the three states of matter

Some attractive forces form between particles during condensing, and many attractive forces are formed during freezing. For this to happen, energy must be transferred from the particles to the surroundings. This is why water vapour turns into water droplets on a cold window, and why you put water in a freezer to make ice.

You can predict the state of a substance if you know its temperature, and its **melting point** and **boiling point**. If the temperature is:

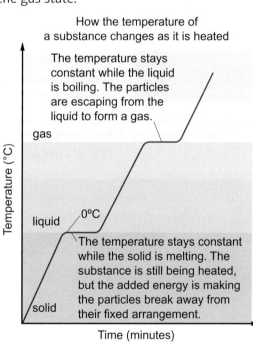

How the temperature of a substance changes as it is heated

The temperature stays constant while the liquid is boiling. The particles are escaping from the liquid to form a gas.

The temperature stays constant while the solid is melting. The substance is still being heated, but the added energy is making the particles break away from their fixed arrangement.

D a heating curve for water

 4 Describe how you can see from a 'heating curve' (such as diagram D) that a substance is changing state.

 5 Explain what happens to the particles when a substance melts.

 6 The melting point of gallium is 29.8 °C and its boiling point is 2204 °C. Predict its state at 25 °C, 100 °C and at 2205 °C.

- below the melting point, the substance is solid
- between the melting point and boiling point, the substance is liquid
- above the boiling point, the substance is gas.

Checkpoint

How confidently can you answer the questions at the top of the previous page?

Strengthen

S1 Draw a diagram to show the states of matter. On your diagram, name each state change and describe what happens to the particles as it happens.

Extend

E1 Explain why the arrangement, movement and energy of particles change during changes of state.

Exam-style question

Exam-style questions will follow on publication of the sample assessment materials by Edexcel.

Please see www.edexcel.com/gcsesci16 for more details.

CC2a Mixtures

Specification reference: C3.1; C3.2

Progression questions

- What is the difference between a pure substance and a mixture?
- What happens to its particles when a solid melts?
- How do melting points allow you to spot the differences between pure substances and mixtures?

A You can tell this gold bar is very nearly pure because of the '999.9' stamped on it. A number lower than 1000 on this 'fineness' scale means it is impure.

The composition (make-up) of a **pure** substance:

- cannot be changed
- is the same in all parts of a piece of the substance.

So, for example, pure gold contains only gold atoms.

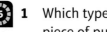 **1** Which type of atoms are found in a piece of pure silver?

 2 A piece of gold is found to be **impure**. Explain what the term 'impure' means.

Gold is an **element** and can be pure, but **compounds** can also be pure. The sugar we use at home is a compound called sucrose. It contains carbon, hydrogen and oxygen atoms chemically bonded together to form sucrose molecules. You cannot change the composition of pure sucrose.

Did you know?

The purest gold ever was produced in 1957 and was 999.999 on the fineness scale.

Gold purity is still often measured on the older carat scale, where 24 carat gold is pure gold.

B Pure sucrose is always sucrose, no matter how finely it is ground down.

A pure substance has the same fixed composition in all its parts and so we can't separate it into other substances using physical methods (such as filtering or picking bits out).

A **mixture** contains elements and/or compounds that are not chemically joined together. You *can* use physical processes to separate mixtures into different substances.

A mixture does not have a fixed composition. For example, air is a mixture of gases. When students sit in a classroom, they use up oxygen and breathe out carbon dioxide and so the composition of the air in the room changes. We still call it 'air', but because air is a mixture its composition can change.

 3 **a** Describe what a mixture of carbon, hydrogen and oxygen might look like.

 b Describe how you would separate marbles from sand.

 4 Oxygen can be removed from air by cooling. Explain why this would not be possible if air were not a mixture.

Melting points

When a solid melts, its particles gain enough energy to overcome the weak forces of attraction between them. They move further away from one another and the solid becomes a liquid. The temperature at which this happens is the **melting point**. This is an example of a **physical property** (how a substance responds to forces and energy).

A pure substance has the same composition in every part of it, and so its physical properties are the same in every part. So, all of a pure substance will melt at the same temperature until all the substance has changed state. The melting point of pure gold is 1063 °C and the melting point of oxygen is −218 °C.

 5 What is the freezing point of pure oxygen?

C this sweet is a mixture and so does not have a sharp melting point

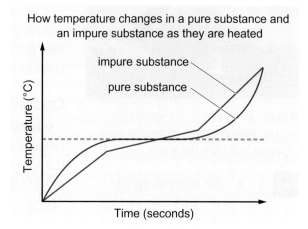

How temperature changes in a pure substance and an impure substance as they are heated

impure substance

pure substance

Temperature (°C)

Time (seconds)

D heating curves for a pure substance and a mixture

The sweet shown in photo C has a liquid centre. The whole sweet melts over a *range* of temperatures and not all the parts melt and become liquid at the same time. This is what happens in mixtures – they do not have fixed, sharp melting points.

Substance	Melting temperatures (°C)
lead–tin alloy	183 to 258
argon	−189
carbon monoxide	−205

6 The table shows some melting temperatures.

a Identify which substances are mixtures and which are pure.

b Sketch a cooling curve for each of the three examples and explain their shapes.

Exam-style question

Exam-style questions will follow on publication of the sample assessment materials by Edexcel.

Please see www.edexcel.com/gcsesci16 for more details.

Checkpoint

How confidently can you answer the questions at the top of the previous page?

Strengthen

S1 List the ways in which pure substances are different from mixtures.

Extend

E1 A piece of gold jewellery is 750 on the fineness scale. Would you expect the jewellery to have a sharp melting temperature? Explain your answer.

CC2b Filtration and crystallisation

Specification reference: C3.3; C0.6

Progression questions

- How can filtration be used to separate mixtures?
- How can crystallisation be used to separate mixtures?
- What are the hazards and risks when separating mixtures by filtration and crystallisation?

A Some whales filter sea water with bristles (called baleen plates) to separate krill from the water.

1 a Give one example of a mixture that can be separated by filtration.

b Explain how this mixture is separated by filtration.

c Describe another type of mixture that can be separated by filtration.

Did you know?

Nearly 4 million tonnes of salt are solution mined in the UK each year.

C Salt can be produced by the evaporation of sea water.

Filters can be used to separate some mixtures. They let smaller pieces or liquids through but trap bigger pieces or **insoluble** substances.

Examples of **filtration** are to be seen all around us. Cars, vacuum cleaners and air-conditioning systems all have filters. Some whales use filters to feed. They open their mouths and take in water. When they close their mouths, they push out the water through filters. Small animals (such as krill) get stuck in the filters and are swallowed.

Crystallisation

A **solution** is a mixture made of **solutes** (dissolved substances) in a liquid called the **solvent**. Solutes can be separated from a solution by evaporating the solvent to leave the solutes behind. This is called **crystallisation**. The process forms solid crystals of various sizes. If the crystals form slowly, the particles have longer to form an ordered pattern and will make larger crystals.

B Crystals in the Giant Crystal Cave in Mexico took over 500 000 years to form.

Table salt is produced from sea water, or is dug out of the ground or extracted using 'solution mining'. In this process water is pumped into layers of salt underground. The resulting salt solution is then heated, which evaporates the solvent and makes the solution more and more salty. Eventually it reaches a point where there is as much salt in the water as can possibly dissolve. This is a **saturated solution** and it contains the maximum amount of solute that can dissolve in that amount of solvent at that temperature. If more water evaporates and/or the solution cools, then some solute leaves the solution and salt crystals form.

Filtration and crystallisation in the lab

To filter a solution in the laboratory, a filter funnel is lined with filter paper that has fine holes in it. The solvent and solute(s) pass through the fine holes to form the **filtrate**. Bits of insoluble substances cannot fit through the holes and so leave a **residue** in the filter paper. A Bunsen burner is then used to evaporate the filtrate carefully. Care must be taken not to overheat the solution once it is saturated, because hot crystals may spit out. Further heating may also cause crystals to change chemically.

i

ii

water vapour

filter paper
suspension
solid residue
filter funnel
filtrate

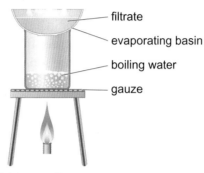
filtrate
evaporating basin
boiling water
gauze

D Laboratory apparatus for (i) filtration and (ii) crystallisation.

In a **risk assessment**, the **hazards** of doing an experiment are identified. A hazard is something that could cause harm. Then ways of reducing the **risk** (chance) of a hazard causing harm are considered.

During crystallisation, the risks from spitting can be reduced by wearing eye protection, removing the Bunsen burner before the solution is completely dry and/or using steam to heat the evaporating basin gently (as above).

7 When a mixture of rock pieces, salt and water is filtered, what will be found as the:

    a filtrate

    b residue?

8 **a** List two of the hazards when carrying out filtration and crystallisation.

    b Explain how the risks from each of your hazards can be reduced.

Exam-style question

Exam-style questions will follow on publication of the sample assessment materials by Edexcel.

Please see www.edexcel.com/gcsesci16 for more details.

2 Give the names of two mixtures that can be separated by crystallisation.

3 In the solution mining of salt, give the names of the:

    a solvent

    b solution

    c solute.

4 When is a solution said to be 'saturated'?

5 Explain why crystals form during crystallisation.

6 Explain why the crystals in photo B are so big.

Checkpoint

How confidently can you answer the questions at the top of the previous page?

Strengthen

S1 Explain how you would separate sand *and* salt from a mixture of the two.

Extend

E1 Scientists looking for new substances in plants grind up the plants with methanol. This solvent dissolves many plant compounds. However, methanol is flammable and toxic (especially if the vapour is inhaled). Large crystals can be made to help scientists work out what the compounds are made of. Explain how you would make plant-compound crystals using methanol.

CC2c Paper chromatography

Specification reference: C3.3; C3.5; C3.6

Progression questions

- How can chromatography be used to separate mixtures?
- What are the differences between mixtures and pure substances on a chromatogram?
- How do you calculate an R_f value?

A Experts restoring an old painting – they need to know what substances were mixed together to produce the paints used by the original artist.

Inks, paints and foods often contain mixtures of coloured compounds. **Chromatography** can be used to find out which coloured compounds the mixture contains. The type of chromatography used to analyse the substances in old oil paintings requires expensive machinery.

Paper chromatography is a simpler technique that works because some compounds dissolve better in a solvent than others. When a solvent moves along a strip of paper, it carries the different substances in the mixture at different speeds, so they are separated. The solvent is called the **mobile phase**. The paper contains the **stationary phase**, through which the solvent and dissolved substances move. The paper with the separated components on it is called a **chromatogram**.

 1 a How many different compounds are in substance X in diagram B?

 b For mixture Y, explain why the green spot is higher than the red spot.

2 Look at diagram B again. Explain why:

 a the labels for substances X, Y and Z are written in pencil, not ink

 b the starting positions for the different substances are above the level of solvent in the container.

 3 One of the coloured compounds in diagram B has an R_f value of 0.1. Explain which compound this is likely to be.

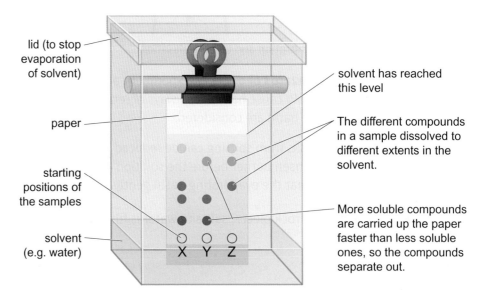

lid (to stop evaporation of solvent)

paper

starting positions of the samples

solvent (e.g. water)

X Y Z

solvent has reached this level

The different compounds in a sample dissolved to different extents in the solvent.

More soluble compounds are carried up the paper faster than less soluble ones, so the compounds separate out.

B paper chromatography

The **R_f value** is the distance the compound has risen divided by the distance the solvent has risen. Both measurements are made from the starting positions of the samples on the paper.

$$R_f = \frac{\text{distance moved by the spot}}{\text{distance moved by the solvent}}$$

The R_f value of a particular compound does not change if the chromatography conditions used remain the same.

Worked example

In diagram B, the pink spots have moved 4 cm and the solvent has moved 10 cm along the paper. Calculate the R_f value of this pink compound:

$R_f = \dfrac{4}{10} = 0.4$ — A compound never rises as fast as the solvent, so R_f values are always less than 1. If you calculate an R_f value bigger than 1, you've made a mistake.

Paper chromatography can be used to:

- distinguish between pure and impure substances
- identify substances by comparing the pattern on the chromatogram with the patterns formed by known substances
- identify substances by calculating their R_f values.

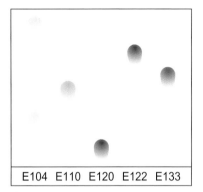

E104 E110 E120 E122 E133

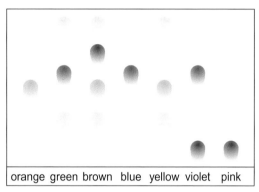

orange green brown blue yellow violet pink

C The chromatogram on the left was done using known substances. The chromatogram on the right shows that the orange and blue sweets contain single dyes.

 4 In diagram B, the yellow spots have moved 9 cm and the solvent has moved 10 cm. Calculate the R_f value of the yellow substance.

5 In diagram C, the chromatogram on the left shows some food dyes found in sweets. The chromatogram on the right shows the results for some sweets.

 a Which sweets contain just one dye?

 b Which dyes are in the yellow sweets?

 c What is the colour of the most soluble dye?

Did you know?

In 1983, many national newspapers paid a lot of money to publish diaries allegedly written by Adolf Hitler. However, scientists used chromatography to analyse the inks in the diaries and found that they were not available during Hitler's lifetime – the diaries were fake.

D Chromatography can be used to help identify substances at crime scenes.

Exam-style question

Exam-style questions will follow on publication of the sample assessment materials by Edexcel.

Please see www.edexcel.com/gcsesci16 for more details.

Checkpoint

How confidently can you answer the questions at the top of the previous page?

Strengthen

S1 The police have taken four orange lipsticks from suspects. Explain the steps needed to find out if one of the lipsticks could have made a mark at a crime scene.

Extend

E1 A laboratory produces a list of R_f values for food colourings. Explain why R_f values are used and what other information is needed for these R_f values to be useful.

CC2d Distillation

Specification reference: C3.3; C0.6

Progression questions

- What is distillation?
- How do simple distillation and fractional distillation differ?
- How would you reduce risks when carrying out a distillation experiment?

A a steam iron

Tap water contains dissolved minerals, especially in hard water areas – tap water is a **mixture**. For some jobs it is best to use pure water (such as for chemical analysis, in car-cooling systems and older steam irons). To make water pure we need to separate it from the dissolved solids. This is done by **distillation**.

1 a What happens to the water in a steam iron when you turn the iron on?

b Explain why some irons may not work well if you use ordinary tap water.

2 In diagram B, what is the hazard if steam escapes from the tube?

3 Suggest a way of improving a simple still so that more of the steam condenses back to water.

When mineral water **evaporates**, only the water turns to a gas (vapour). The solid minerals, which have much higher boiling points, are left behind. The water vapour (steam) is pure. If the vapour is then **condensed**, it turns back to liquid water again – the liquid water will now be pure. This combination of evaporation followed by condensation is called distillation. The apparatus used is called a **still**.

Diagram B shows a simple method for distilling. Water is heated in the conical flask and the vapour travels along the delivery tube, where it condenses. This method is not very efficient because much of the vapour is lost.

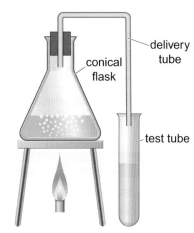

B a simple still

The type of still shown in diagram C is more efficient. The condenser keeps the tube cool, so that almost all of the vapour condenses and turns into a liquid.

4 Explain how the still in diagram C can be used to purify water.

5 Explain how:

a the condenser reduces the risk of hot vapour escaping

b the safety of the method is improved by using anti-bumping granules.

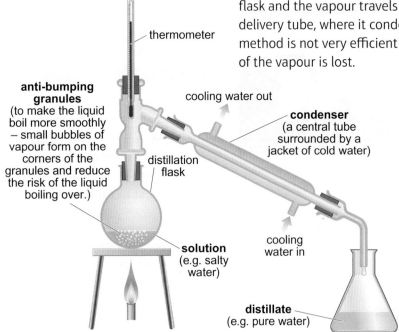

thermometer

anti-bumping granules (to make the liquid boil more smoothly – small bubbles of vapour form on the corners of the granules and reduce the risk of the liquid boiling over.)

cooling water out

condenser (a central tube surrounded by a jacket of cold water)

distillation flask

solution (e.g. salty water)

cooling water in

distillate (e.g. pure water)

C distillation apparatus

Fractional distillation

Distillation can also be used to separate two or more liquids. This works because some liquids boil more easily than others. Liquids with lower boiling points evaporate more easily than others, and will turn into a vapour first. This is called **fractional distillation**, because the original mixture will be split into several parts, or fractions. The first fraction to be collected contains the liquid with the lowest boiling point. The fractions could be pure liquids, or may still be mixtures.

Fractional distillation can be used:

- to separate the different products in crude oil
- to make alcoholic drinks such as whisky and vodka
- to separate out the gases in the air, after the air has been cooled and turned into a liquid at −200 °C.

Diagram D shows how to separate liquids more efficiently. A column is fixed above the distillation flask. The hot vapour rises up the column. At first, the vapour condenses when it hits the cool glass and drips back down into the flask. As the column gradually heats up, there will be a temperature gradient – it will be hottest at the bottom and the temperature will drop as you go further up the column. The fraction with the lowest boiling point will reach the top of the column first and the vapour will then pass into the condenser. If you keep heating, fractions with higher boiling points will then rise up the column and can be collected later.

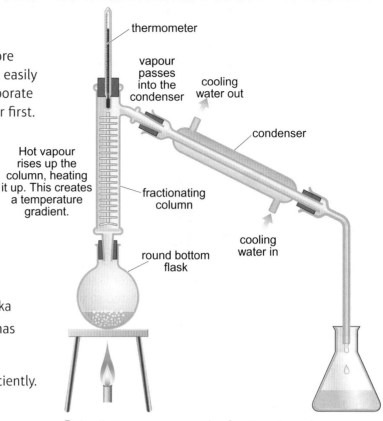

D distillation apparatus with a fractionating column

 6 Compare and contrast simple and fractional distillation.

 7 Explain why a liquid with a lower boiling point will reach the top of a fractionating column more quickly than one with a higher boiling point.

Did you know?

The vacuum flask that we now use to keep drinks hot was originally used to keep liquid air *cold*. It was designed by James Dewar in 1892.

Exam-style question

Exam-style questions will follow on publication of the sample assessment materials by Edexcel.

Please see www.edexcel.com/gcsesci16 for more details.

Checkpoint

How confidently can you answer the questions at the top of the previous page?

Strengthen

S1 Explain what distillation is and how the distillation apparatus (the still) works. Use a labelled diagram to make your explanation clear.

S2 Explain the safety precautions you need to take when carrying out distillation in a laboratory.

Extend

E1 Pure ethanol ('alcohol') boils at 78.5 °C. Explain how a 50:50 mixture of ethanol and water can be separated by fractional distillation.

E2 Suggest why the boiling point of the starting liquid will change with time.

CC2e Drinking water

Specification reference: C3.4; C3.8; C0.6

Progression questions

- How would you choose which method to use to separate a mixture?
- How is drinking water produced?
- Why must water used in chemical analysis be pure?

A Personal water purifiers filter water to make it safe to drink.

 1 Explain how pure water is produced using the apparatus shown in diagram B.

 2 Suggest why the simple distillation of sea water may be used to provide drinking water in oil-rich coastal countries.

C A cloudy white precipitate forming during a chemical analysis.

About 97% of the Earth's water is in the oceans. The concentration of dissolved salts in sea water is far too high for us to drink safely. Producing pure water from sea water is called **desalination** and can be achieved using **simple distillation**.

Purifying sea water

Water is separated from dissolved salts using simple distillation. Sea water is heated so that water vapour leaves it quickly. This vapour is then cooled and condensed, forming water without the dissolved salts.

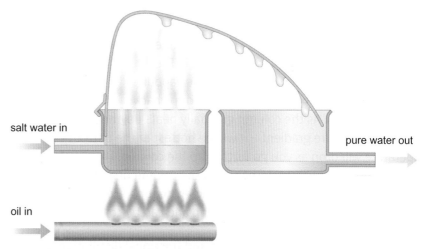

salt water in

pure water out

oil in

B Simple distillation of sea water using oil as a fuel.

A lot of energy must be transferred to sea water during simple distillation, so it is not usually a suitable method for producing large volumes of drinking water. It is mainly carried out on a large scale where energy resources are cheap or plentiful, and where there is an abundant supply of sea water.

Water for chemical analysis

Chemical analysis involves using chemical reactions or sensitive machines to identify and measure the substances in a sample. The water used for chemical analysis should not contain any dissolved salts, otherwise incorrect results will be obtained. Tap water contains small amounts of dissolved salts, which may react to form unexpected cloudy **precipitates**. These may hide the correct result of the analysis. Also, the machines used for analysis may detect the salts, again leading to an incorrect conclusion.

 3 Explain why distilled water is more suitable than tap water for doing a chemical analysis.

Water for drinking

In the UK, the raw material for producing drinking water comes from rivers, lakes or **aquifers** (underground rocks containing groundwater). The water in these sources is often stored in reservoirs, which are artificial lakes produced by building a dam across a valley. Fresh water from these sources contains:

- objects such as leaves and twigs
- small insoluble particles such as grit and silt
- soluble substances, including salts, pesticides and fertilisers
- bacteria and other microorganisms that may be harmful to health.

Different steps are needed to deal with these impurities. They include screening using a sieve, **sedimentation** (in which small particles are allowed to settle out) and filtration using tanks containing beds of sand and gravel. Chlorine is added in a process called **chlorination**. Chlorine kills microorganisms in the treated water.

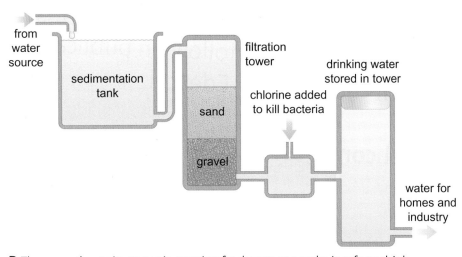

D These are the main stages in treating fresh water to make it safe to drink.

 5 a Describe how water is treated to deal with leaves and twigs, grit and silt, and with microorganisms.

 b Identify the stage missing from diagram D and draw a labelled diagram to show it.

 6 Suggest why chemical reactions, rather than separation methods, are used to remove harmful substances dissolved in drinking water in the UK.

Exam-style question

Exam-style questions will follow on publication of the sample assessment materials by Edexcel.

Please see www.edexcel.com/gcsesci16 for more details.

 4 Explain why it may not be safe to drink water straight from a river.

Did you know?

Only about 2.5% of the Earth's water is fresh water. Of that, only 0.3% is in rivers and lakes – the rest is in icecaps, glaciers and ground water.

Checkpoint

How confidently can you answer the questions at the top of the previous page?

Strengthen

S1 Draw flowcharts to describe two ways in which water can be made fit to drink.

Extend

E1 A bottle of water has a label saying 'Suitable for chemical analysis'. Describe how this water has been produced.

E2 Explain how you would check to see if this water really is suitable for analysis.

Term 1

Exam-style questions and sample student answers with expert commentary and exam tips will follow on publication of the sample assessment materials by Edexcel.

Please see www.edexcel.com/gcsesci16 for more details.

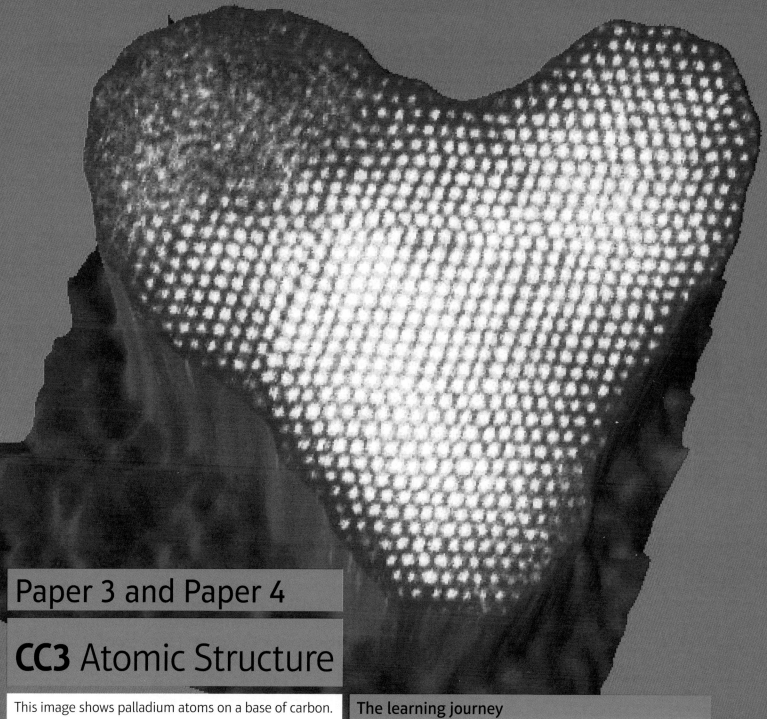

Paper 3 and Paper 4

CC3 Atomic Structure

This image shows palladium atoms on a base of carbon. According to the scientists who produced it, Zhiwei Wand and David Pearmain, although they had watched with love, they had nothing to do with the spontaneous formation of the heart shape. Unfortunately this atomic valentine, being only 8 nanometres (0.000000008 metres) across, is far too small to see even with the strongest light microscope. It may, however, help to explain the nature of matter, which is central to understanding the properties of materials and the chemical reactions that form new substances. In this unit you will find out more about atoms and their structure.

The learning journey

Previously you will have learnt at KS3:

* about the particle model of matter
* how Dalton's ideas about atoms helped to explain the properties of matter
* how elements are arranged in the periodic table.

In this unit you will learn:

* how our ideas about atoms have changed
* what a relative atomic mass is
* **H** how to calculate relative atomic mass for an element.

CC3a Structure of an atom

Specification reference: C1.1; C1.2; C1.3; C1.4; C1.5

Progression questions

- How has the model of the atom changed over the last 200 years?
- How do the parts of atoms compare with each other?
- Why do atoms have no overall charge?

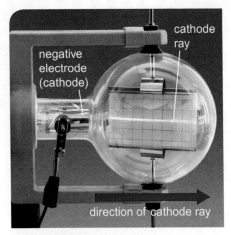

A a cathode ray tube

 1 What are atoms?

 2 Which of Dalton's ideas about particles is supported by the image of palladium atoms on the previous page?

In 1805 the English chemist John Dalton (1766–1844) published his atomic theory that said:

- all matter is made up of tiny particles called **atoms**
- atoms are tiny, hard spheres that cannot be broken down into smaller parts
- atoms cannot be created or destroyed
- the atoms in an **element** are all identical (but each element has its own type of atom).

Dalton's ideas helped to explain some of the properties of matter. However, experiments towards the end of the nineteenth century suggested that atoms contain even smaller particles.

When a high voltage is applied to a glass tube that has most of the air removed, glowing rays are seen. Some scientists thought that these 'cathode rays' were atoms leaving the negative electrode. In 1897, JJ Thomson (1856–1940) investigated the mass of the particles in the rays and found that they were about 1800 times lighter than the lightest atom (hydrogen). Cathode rays, therefore, did not contain atoms but **subatomic particles**, which we now call **electrons**.

The structure of atoms

Scientists have now worked out that atoms are made up of electrons together with heavier subatomic particles called **protons** and **neutrons**. All these particles have very, very small masses and electric charges. So, rather than use their actual masses and charges, it is easier to describe them by looking at their **relative masses** and **relative charges** compared to a proton. For example, if we say the mass of a proton is '1' then anything else that has the same mass is also '1'.

Did you know?

The actual mass of a proton is 0.000 000 000 000 000 000 000 001 67 g (1.67×10^{-24} g).

Subatomic particle	Relative charge	Relative mass
proton	+1 (positive)	1
electron	−1 (negative)	1/1835 (negligible)
neutron	0 (no charge)	1

B relative masses and relative charges of subatomic particles

At the centre of all atoms is a tiny **nucleus** containing protons and neutrons. This is surrounded by fast moving electrons arranged in **electron shells** at different distances from the nucleus.

 3 Which subatomic particle has the lowest mass?

Atoms in elements always have equal numbers of protons and electrons and so have no overall charge, because the charges cancel out.

Diagram C shows two ways of modelling a beryllium atom. The three-dimensional model attempts to show how we imagine electrons to move.

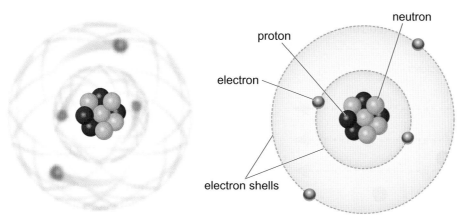

neutron
proton
electron
electron shells

C The 'target diagram' on the right shows the arrangement of the electrons more clearly.

Models of atoms help us to understand their structure – but most models don't really give a correct impression of scale. The overall diameter of an atom can be 100 000 times the diameter of its nucleus.

D If an atom could be made the size of the Lord's cricket ground, its nucleus would be about the size of this dot ●. Most of an atom is empty space.

Exam-style question

Exam-style questions will follow on publication of the sample assessment materials by Edexcel.

Please see www.edexcel.com/gcsesci16 for more details.

4 How many protons, neutrons and electrons are in a beryllium atom?

5 A lithium atom has 3 protons, 4 neutrons and 3 electrons.

a Draw a diagram of this atom.

b Why is this atom neutral?

c How many electrons would be in an atom that has 17 protons?

Checkpoint

How confidently can you answer the questions at the top of the previous page?

Strengthen

S1 Draw an atom and label it to describe the arrangement and properties of its subatomic particles.

Extend

E1 Figure E (below) shows what happens when the three subatomic particles are fired through an electric field.

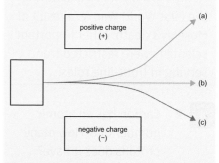

positive charge (+)

negative charge (−)

Name each particle a, b and c. Explain your answer.

CC3b Atomic number and mass number

Specification reference: C1.6; C1.7; C1.8; C1.10

Progression questions

- Why is most of the mass of an atom found in its nucleus?
- What does the atomic number tell you about an element?
- How can you calculate the numbers of protons, neutrons and electrons in atoms?

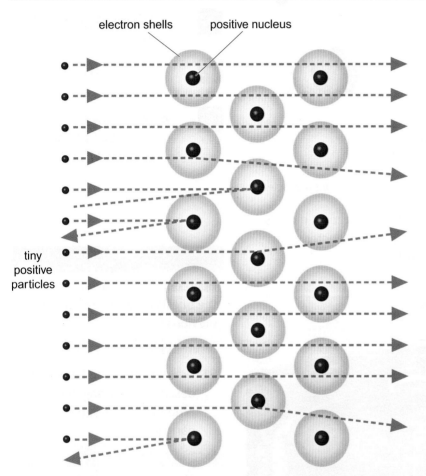

electron shells   positive nucleus

tiny positive particles

A Rutherford's scattering experiments suggested a nuclear atomic model.

The nuclear atom

In 1909, Ernest Rutherford (1871–1937) was working with others to investigate the structure of atoms. In one experiment, tiny positive particles were fired at a thin gold foil. To everyone's surprise most of the particles passed straight through the gold foil, with a few being deflected and a very small number bouncing back. Rutherford explained this by suggesting that atoms are mostly empty space, with a small positive central nucleus that contains most of the mass.

 1 a Where is most of the mass of an atom?

 b Explain how the experiment in diagram A suggests that atoms are mostly empty space.

Atomic number

The elements in the **periodic table** were originally placed in order of the masses of their atoms. However, this caused some elements to be grouped with others that had very different properties. So a few elements were swapped round to make sure that those with similar properties were grouped together, even if it meant that they were no longer in the correct order of mass.

Did you know?

Henry Moseley was killed during the First World War. As a result of Moseley's death, other important scientists were restricted from serving in front-line roles.

 2 Carbon has an atomic number of 6. How many protons does it have?

Experiments by Henry Moseley (1887–1915) in 1913 confirmed that the rearranged order of elements in the table was actually correct. He showed that they were in order of the amount of positive charge in the nucleus. The proton was discovered about five years later. The modern periodic table places the elements in order of the number of protons in their atoms. This is the **atomic number** and it is this that defines an element – all the atoms of a particular element have the same unique atomic number.

3 Use a periodic table to find:

a the number of protons and electrons in atoms of:

   i nitrogen   **ii** potassium

b two elements whose atomic mass order does not match their atomic number order.

4 In terms of structure, what do all atoms of a certain element have in common?

Mass number

The mass of an electron is described as 'negligible' – it is so small that it can be ignored. This explains why the nucleus of any atom contains nearly all its mass. For this reason the total number of protons and neutrons in an atom is called its **mass number**.

A mass number is represented by the symbol A and an atomic number by the symbol Z. These numbers are written next to an element's symbol as shown in diagram B.

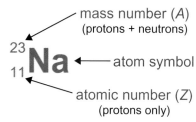

mass number (A)
(protons + neutrons)

$$^{23}_{11}\text{Na}$$

atom symbol

atomic number (Z)
(protons only)

B This is how scientists write the atomic number and the mass number for a sodium atom. It shows that the atom contains 11 protons and 12 neutrons in its nucleus.

5 How many protons, neutrons and electrons are in the atom $^{27}_{13}\text{Al}$? Explain how you worked out your answer.

6 A manganese atom has 25 protons, 30 neutrons and 25 electrons. Show this information using the form shown in diagram B.

7 Look at the 'Did you know?' box on this page. Which subatomic particle does a hydrogen atom *not* have? Explain your reasoning.

Exam-style question

Exam-style questions will follow on publication of the sample assessment materials by Edexcel.

Please see www.edexcel.com/gcsesci16 for more details.

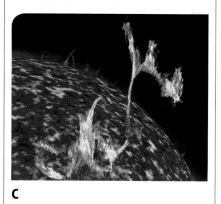
Checkpoint

How confidently can you answer the questions at the top of the previous page?

Strengthen

S1 An atom can be represented in the form $^{65}_{29}\text{Cu}$. What does this tell you about this atom?

Extend

E1 Formulae can be written to connect the atomic number, mass number, and numbers of protons, electrons and neutrons in atoms.

For example:

atomic number = protons

Write formulae that connect the other four numbers.

Term 1

Exam-style questions and sample student answers with expert commentary and exam tips will follow on publication of the sample assessment materials by Edexcel.

Please see www.edexcel.com/gcsesci16 for more details.

CP1 Motion

Penguins cannot climb. They get onto the ice by accelerating to a high speed under the water. As they move upwards out of the water, gravity pulls on them and they slow down. But if they are swimming fast enough they land on the ice before they stop moving.

In this unit you will learn about quantities that have directions (such as forces). You will find out how to calculate speeds and accelerations, and how to represent changes in distance moved and speed on graphs.

The learning journey

Previously you will have learnt at KS3:

- what forces are and the effects of balanced and unbalanced forces
- how average speed, distance and time are related
- how to represent a journey on a distance-time graph.

In this unit you will learn:

- the difference between vector and scalar quantities
- how to calculate speed and acceleration
- how to represent journeys on distance/time and velocity/time graphs
- how to use graphs to calculate speed, acceleration and distance travelled.

CP1a Vectors and scalars

Specification reference: P1.1; P1.2; P1.3; P1.10

Progression questions

- What are vector and scalar quantities?
- What are some examples of scalar quantities and their corresponding vector quantities?
- What is the connection between the speed, velocity and acceleration of an object?

A The person in the air stays there because of the force provided by the jets of water.

1 Upthrust is a force that helps objects float. Sketch one of the boats in photo A and add arrows to show two forces on the boat acting in a vertical direction.

2 Describe the differences between mass and weight.

3 Explain why we say that displacement is a vector quantity.

4 Runners in a 400 m race complete one circuit of an athletics track. What is their displacement at the end of the race?

The **force** needed to keep the person in photo A in the air depends on his **weight**. Weight is a force that acts towards the centre of the Earth. All forces have both a **magnitude** (size) and a direction, and are measured in newtons (N).

Quantities that have both size and direction are **vector quantities**. So forces are vectors. Forces are often shown on diagrams using arrows, with longer arrows representing larger forces.

The weight of the person in photo A depends on his **mass**. Mass measures the amount of matter in something and does not have a direction. Quantities that do not have a direction are called **scalar quantities**. Other scalar quantities include **distance**, **speed**, energy and time.

Displacement is the distance covered in a straight line, and has a direction. The displacement at the end of a journey is usually less than the distance travelled because of the turns or bends in the journey.

B The bend in the road means that the distance the cyclists cover is greater than their final displacement.

The speed of an object tells you how far it moves in a certain time. **Velocity** is speed in a particular direction. For example a car may have a velocity of 20 m/s northwards.

D These skaters maintain a constant speed around the bend, but their velocity is changing.

Other vector quantities include:

• **acceleration** – a measure of how fast velocity is changing
• **momentum** – a combination of mass and velocity.

Exam-style question

Exam-style questions will follow on publication of the sample assessment materials by Edexcel.

Please see www.edexcel.com/gcsesci16 for more details.

7 **5** Look at photo B. Explain why the cyclists' velocity will change even if they maintain the same speed.

8 **6** A student draws the diagram below. Explain what is wrong with it.

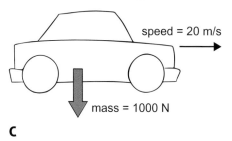

C

Checkpoint

How confidently can you answer the questions at the top of the previous page?

Strengthen

S1 Sally walks 1 km from her home to school. When she arrives, she tells her science teacher 'My velocity to school this morning was 15 minutes'. What would her teacher say?

S2 Explain the difference between displacement and distance, and between speed and velocity. Give an example of each.

Extend

E1 A car is going around a roundabout. Explain why it is accelerating even if it is moving at a constant speed.

CP1b Distance/time graphs

Specification reference: P1.4; P1.5; P1.9

Progression questions

- How do you use the formula relating average speed, distance and time?
- In metres per second, what are the typical speeds that someone might move at during the course of a day?
- How do you represent journeys on a distance/time graph?

A *ThrustSSC* broke the land speed record in 1997 at a speed of 1228 km/h (341 m/s). This was faster than the speed of sound (which is approximately 330 m/s).

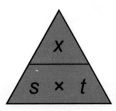

B This formula triangle can help you to rearrange the formula for speed (*s*), where *x* is used to represent distance and *t* represents time. Cover up the quantity you want to calculate and write what you see on the right of the = sign.

The speed of an object tells you how quickly it travels a certain distance. Common units for speed are metres per second (m/s), kilometres per hour (km/h) and miles per hour (mph).

The speed during a journey can change, and the **average speed** is worked out from the total distance travelled and the total time taken. The **instantaneous speed** is the speed at a particular point in a journey.

Speed can be calculated using the following formula:

$$\text{(average) speed (m/s)} = \frac{\text{distance (m)}}{\text{time taken (s)}}$$

The formula can be rearranged to calculate the distance travelled from the speed and the time.

$$\underset{\text{(m)}}{\text{distance travelled}} = \underset{\text{(m/s)}}{\text{average speed}} \times \underset{\text{(s)}}{\text{time}}$$

Worked example W1

How far would *ThrustSSC* have travelled in 5 seconds during its record-breaking run?

distance = average speed × time

= 341 m/s × 5 s

= 1705 m

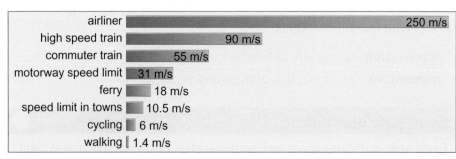

C some typical speeds

 1 A car travels 3000 m in 2 minutes (120 seconds). Calculate its speed in m/s.

 2 Look at diagram C. How far does a high speed train travel in 10 minutes?

Distance/time graphs

A journey can be represented on a **distance/time graph**. Since time and distance are used to calculate speed, the graph can tell us various things about speed:

- horizontal lines mean the object is stationary (its distance from the starting point is not changing)
- straight, sloping lines mean the object is travelling at constant speed
- the steeper the line, the faster the object is travelling
- the speed is calculated from the **gradient** of the line.

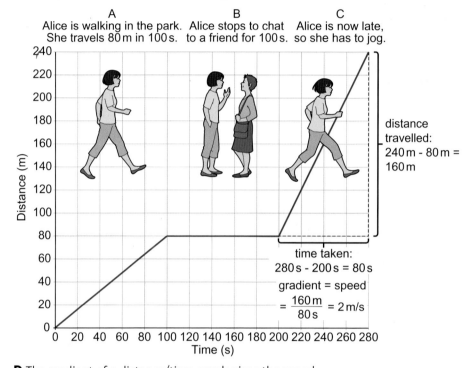

A Alice is walking in the park. She travels 80 m in 100 s.
B Alice stops to chat to a friend for 100 s.
C Alice is now late, so she has to jog.

distance travelled: 240 m - 80 m = 160 m

time taken: 280 s - 200 s = 80 s

gradient = speed
$$= \frac{160\,m}{80\,s} = 2\,m/s$$

D The gradient of a distance/time graph gives the speed.

Worked example W2

In graph D, what is Alice's speed for part C of her walk?

$$gradient = \frac{\text{vertical difference between two points on a graph}}{\text{horizontal difference between the same two points}}$$

$$= \frac{240\ m - 80\ m}{280\ s - 200\ s}$$

Make sure you take the starting value away from the end value each time.

$$speed = \frac{160\ m}{80\ s}$$

$$speed = 2\ m/s$$

Exam-style question

Exam-style questions will follow on publication of the sample assessment materials by Edexcel.

Please see www.edexcel.com/gcsesci16 for more details.

3 Look at graph D. Calculate Alice's speed for:

  a part A on the graph

  b part B on the graph.

4 If Alice had not stopped to chat but had walked at her initial speed for 280 s, how far would she have travelled?

Checkpoint

How confidently can you answer the questions at the top of the previous page?

Strengthen

S1 A peregrine falcon flies at 50 m/s for 7 seconds. How far does it fly?

S2 Zahir starts a race fast, then gets a stitch and has to stop. When he starts running again he goes more slowly than before. Sketch a distance/time graph to show Zahir's race if he runs at a constant speed in each section of the race.

Extend

E1 Look at question S2. Zahir's speeds are 3 m/s for 60 seconds, 2 m/s for 90 seconds and his rest lasted for 30 seconds. Plot a distance/time graph on graph paper to show his race.

CP1c Acceleration

Specification reference: P1.6; P1.7; P1.11

Progression questions

- How do you calculate accelerations from a change in velocity and a time?
- How are acceleration, initial velocity, final velocity and distance related?
- What is the acceleration of free fall?

piston catapult

A A fighter plane can accelerate from 0 to 80 m/s (180 mph) in 2 seconds.

Fighter planes taking off from aircraft carriers use a catapult to help them to accelerate to flying speed.

A change in velocity is called acceleration. Acceleration is a vector quantity – it has a size (magnitude) and a direction. If a moving object changes its velocity or direction, then it is accelerating.

The acceleration tells you the change in velocity each second, so the units of acceleration are metres per second per second. This is written as m/s² (metres per second squared). An acceleration of 10 m/s² means that each second the velocity increases by 10 m/s.

 1 How are velocity and acceleration connected?

Acceleration is calculated using the following formula:

$$\text{acceleration (m/s}^2) = \frac{\text{change in velocity (m/s)}}{\text{time taken (s)}}$$

This can also be written as:

$$a = \frac{v - u}{t}$$

where a is the acceleration

v is the final velocity

u is the initial velocity

t is the time taken for the change in velocity.

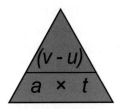

B This triangle can help you to rearrange the formula.

Worked example W1

An airliner's velocity changes from 0 m/s to 60 m/s in 20 seconds. What is its acceleration?

$$a = \frac{v - u}{t}$$

$$= \frac{60 \text{ m/s} - 0 \text{ m/s}}{20 \text{ s}}$$

$$= 3 \text{ m/s}^2$$

 2 Calculate the take-off acceleration of the fighter plane in photo A.

Acceleration does not always mean getting faster. An acceleration can also cause an object to get slower. This is sometimes called a **deceleration**, and the acceleration will have a negative value.

 3 A car slows down from 25 m/s to 10 m/s in 5 seconds. Calculate its acceleration.

Acceleration can be related to initial velocity, final velocity and distance travelled by this formula:

(final velocity)² – (initial velocity)² = 2 × acceleration × distance
    (m/s)²   (m/s)²   (m/s²)   (m)

This can also be written as $v^2 - u^2 = 2 \times a \times x$, where x represents distance.

Worked example W2

A car travelling at 15 m/s accelerates at 1.5 m/s² over a distance of 50 m. Calculate its final velocity.

$v^2 = (2 \times a \times x) + u^2$

$\quad = (2 \times 1.5 \text{ m/s}^2 \times 50 \text{ m}) + (15 \text{ m/s} \times 15 \text{ m/s})$

$v^2 = 375 \text{ (m/s)}^2$

$v = \sqrt{375} \text{ (m/s)}^2$

$\quad = 19.4 \text{ m/s}$

 4 A cyclist accelerates from 2 m/s to 8 m/s with an acceleration of 1.5 m/s². How far did she travel while she was accelerating?

Use the formula $x = \dfrac{v^2 - u^2}{2 \times a}$.

Acceleration due to gravity

An object in free fall is moving downwards because of the force of gravity acting on it. If there are no other forces (such as air resistance), the acceleration due to gravity is 9.8 m/s². This is represented by the symbol g, and is often rounded to 10 m/s² in calculations.

5 Look at photo C.

 a Calculate the acceleration on the ejecting pilot in m/s².

 b How does this compare to everyday accelerations?

Exam-style question

Exam-style questions will follow on publication of the sample assessment materials by Edexcel.

Please see www.edexcel.com/gcsesci16 for more details.

C

Checkpoint

How confidently can you answer the questions at the top of the previous page?

Strengthen

S1 Explain how positive, negative and zero accelerations change the velocity of a moving object.

S2 A car travelling at 40 m/s comes to a halt in 8 seconds. What is the car's acceleration and how far does it travel while it is stopping?

Extend

E1 A train is travelling at 35 m/s. It slows down with an acceleration of –0.5 m/s². How much time does it take to stop and how far does it travel while it is stopping?

CP1d Velocity/time graphs

Specification reference: P1.8

Progression questions

- How do you compare accelerations on a velocity/time graph?
- How can you calculate acceleration from a velocity/time graph?
- How can you use a velocity/time graph to work out the total distance travelled?

A Top Fuel dragsters can reach velocities of 150 m/s (335 mph) in only 4 seconds.

In a drag race, cars accelerate in a straight line over a short course of only a few hundred metres.

The changing velocity of a dragster during a race can be shown using a **velocity/time graph**.

On a velocity/time graph:

- a horizontal line means the object is travelling at constant velocity
- a sloping line shows that the object is accelerating. The steeper the line, the greater the acceleration. If the line slopes down to the right, the object is decelerating (slowing down). You can find the acceleration of an object from the gradient of the line on a velocity/time graph.
- a negative velocity (a line below the horizontal axis) shows the object moving in the opposite direction.

Graph C is a simplified velocity/time graph for a dragster. It shows the car driving slowly to the start line, waiting for the signal, and then racing.

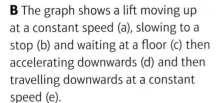

B The graph shows a lift moving up at a constant speed (a), slowing to a stop (b) and waiting at a floor (c) then accelerating downwards (d) and then travelling downwards at a constant speed (e).

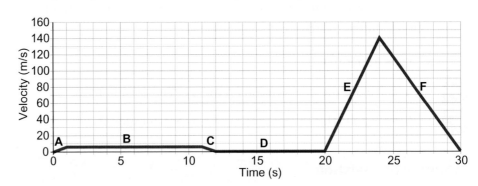

C simplified velocity/time graph for a drag race

 1 What does a horizontal line on a velocity/time graph tell you about an object's velocity?

2 **a** In which part of graph C is the dragster travelling at a constant velocity?

 b In which part of the graph does the dragster have its greatest acceleration?

 c Which part(s) of the graph show that the dragster is slowing down?

 3 Look at graph C. Calculate the acceleration during part F of the journey.

Calculating distance travelled from a graph

The area under a velocity/time graph is the distance the object has travelled (distance is calculated by multiplying a velocity and a time). In graph D, the distance travelled in the first 5 seconds is the area of a rectangle. The distance travelled in the next 5 seconds is found by splitting the shape into a triangle and a rectangle, and finding their areas separately.

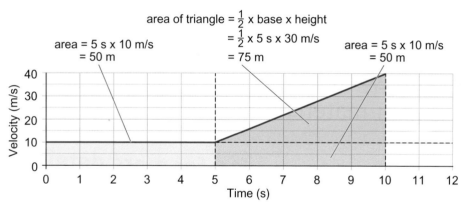

D

The total distance travelled by the object in graph D is the sum of all the areas.

total distance travelled = 50 m + 50 m + 75 m = 175 m

4 Look at graph C. The dragster travels at 5 m/s as it approaches the start line.

 a How far does it travel to get to the start line?

 b What is the distance travelled by the dragster during the race and slowing down afterwards?

 5 Mel draws a graph showing a bus journey through town. Explain why this should be called a speed/time graph, not a velocity/time graph.

Exam-style question

Exam-style questions will follow on publication of the sample assessment materials by Edexcel.

Please see www.edexcel.com/gcsesci16 for more details.

Checkpoint

How confidently can you answer the questions at the top of the previous page?

Strengthen

S1 Table E below gives some data for a train journey. Draw a velocity/time graph from this and join the points with straight lines. Label your graph with all the things you can tell from it. Show your working for any calculations you do.

Time (s)	Velocity (m/s)
0	0
20	10
30	30
60	30
120	0

E

Extend

E1 In a fitness test, students run up and down the sports hall. They have to run faster after each time they turn around. Sketch a velocity/time graph for 4 lengths of the hall, if each length is run at a constant speed.

Term 1

Exam-style questions and sample student answers with expert commentary and exam tips will follow on publication of the sample assessment materials by Edexcel.

Please see www.edexcel.com/gcsesci16 for more details.

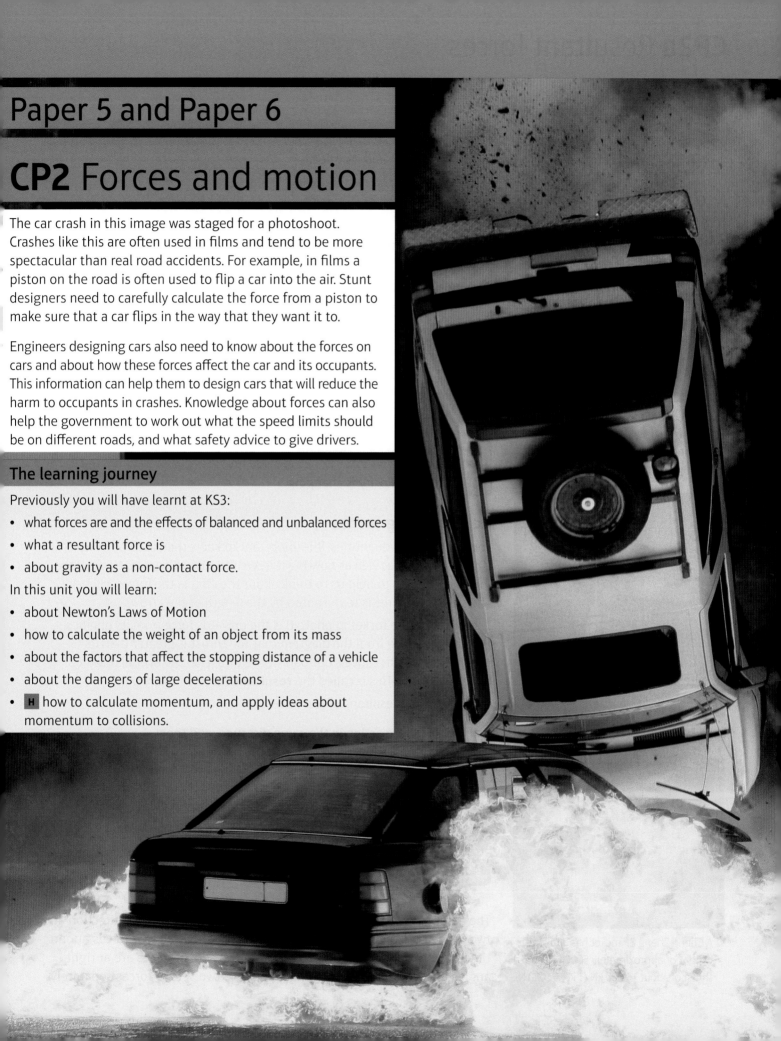

Paper 5 and Paper 6

CP2 Forces and motion

The car crash in this image was staged for a photoshoot. Crashes like this are often used in films and tend to be more spectacular than real road accidents. For example, in films a piston on the road is often used to flip a car into the air. Stunt designers need to carefully calculate the force from a piston to make sure that a car flips in the way that they want it to.

Engineers designing cars also need to know about the forces on cars and about how these forces affect the car and its occupants. This information can help them to design cars that will reduce the harm to occupants in crashes. Knowledge about forces can also help the government to work out what the speed limits should be on different roads, and what safety advice to give drivers.

The learning journey

Previously you will have learnt at KS3:

- what forces are and the effects of balanced and unbalanced forces
- what a resultant force is
- about gravity as a non-contact force.

In this unit you will learn:

- about Newton's Laws of Motion
- how to calculate the weight of an object from its mass
- about the factors that affect the stopping distance of a vehicle
- about the dangers of large decelerations
- **H** how to calculate momentum, and apply ideas about momentum to collisions.

CP2a Resultant forces

Specification reference: P1.12

Progression questions

- What is the difference between the speed of an object and its velocity?
- How do we represent all the forces acting on an object?
- How do we calculate resultant forces?

A A 'wall of death' is a small arena with almost vertical sides. Motorcyclists ride around the walls, and won't fall as long as they keep moving!

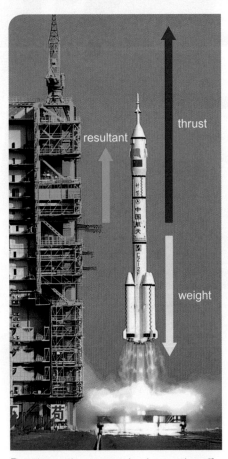

B A Chang Zheng 2F rocket has a take-off weight of approximately 5000 kN, and thrust of about 13 000 kN (1 kN = 1000 N).

Scalars and vectors

The motorcyclist in photo A is moving at a constant **speed** but his **velocity** is changing all the time. This is because velocity is a **vector quantity**. It has a direction as well as a magnitude (size). Speed is a **scalar quantity**. It only has a magnitude.

When an object changes its velocity, it is accelerating. As **acceleration** is a change in a vector quantity (velocity), acceleration is also a vector.

 1 A car is driving around a roundabout at 20 km/h. Explain whether or not:

      a its speed is changing

     b its velocity is changing.

Representing forces

Forces are vector quantities. It is important to know the direction in which a force is acting, as well as how big it is. We can draw diagrams to show the forces on objects to help us to think about the effects the forces will have. The size of the force is represented by the length of the arrows.

The thrust on the rocket in photo B is the upwards force from its engines. You can easily see from the diagram that the thrust is greater than its weight. The weight cancels out part of the thrust, so the overall upwards force is 8000 kN. This is called the **resultant force** on the rocket.

To work out the resultant of two forces:

- if the forces are acting in the same direction, add them
- if they are acting in opposite directions (as in photo B), subtract one from the other.

 2 a A cyclist is riding along a flat road without pedalling. The air resistance is 10 N and friction is 5 N. What is the resultant force on the bike?

      b What is the resultant force if the cyclist is pedalling with a force of 25 N?

The aeroplane in photo C has two forces acting in the vertical direction and two in the horizontal. We do not have to think about all four forces at one time to work out a resultant, because the two sets of forces are at right angles to each other. We can think about the two sets of forces separately.

C

3 Calculate the resultant force on the aeroplane in photo C in the:

a vertical direction

b horizontal direction.

4 In photo C, are the forces balanced or unbalanced in the:

a vertical direction

b horizontal direction?

If the resultant of all the forces on an object is zero, we say the forces are **balanced**. If there is a non-zero resultant force on an object, the forces are **unbalanced**.

D What are the forces on this diver?

Exam-style question

Exam-style questions will follow on publication of the sample assessment materials by Edexcel.

Please see www.edexcel.com/gcsesci16 for more details.

Checkpoint

How confidently can you answer the questions at the top of the previous page?

Strengthen

S1 Draw a concept map to show what you know about forces.

Extend

E1 Calculate the resultant force on the diver in photo D in the vertical direction and in the horizontal direction.

E2 Draw a diagram of the diver and add force arrows to show the two resultant forces.

CP2b Newton's First Law

Specification reference: P1.12; P1.16; P1.17

Progression questions

- What happens to the motion of an object when the forces on it are balanced?
- What can happen to the motion of an object when there is a resultant force on it?
- **H** What is centripetal force?

A Human cannonballs are propelled using unbalanced forces from compressed air or springs – not using explosives!

Sir Isaac Newton (1642–1727) worked out three 'laws' of motion that describe how forces affect the movement of objects.

Newton's First Law of motion can be written as:

- a moving object will continue to move at the same speed and direction unless an external force acts on it
- a stationary object will remain at rest unless an external force acts on it.

It is the overall resultant force that is important when you are looking at how the velocity of an object changes. Balanced forces (zero resultant force) will not change the velocity of an object. Unbalanced forces (non-zero resultant force) will change the speed and/or direction of an object.

 1 a What is the resultant force on the human cannonball in the vertical direction when she is flying through the air?

 b How will this resultant force affect her velocity?

2 Look at photo C on the previous page again. Explain how the velocity of the aeroplane will change in the:

 a vertical direction

 b horizontal direction.

The ice yacht in photo B is not changing speed in the vertical direction. Its weight is balanced by an upwards force from the ice.

3 A sailing boat has a forwards force of 300 N from the wind in its sails. It is travelling at a constant speed.

 a What is the total force acting backwards on the sailing boat? Explain your answer.

b The ice yacht in photo B has the same force from its sails. Explain why its velocity will be increasing.

B An ice yacht can go much faster than a sailing boat in the same wind conditions.

H Circular motion

C This fairground ride is accelerating the people in the chairs.

An object moving in a circle has changing velocity, even though its speed remains the same. The resultant force that causes the change in direction is called the **centripetal force**, and acts towards the centre of the circle. In photo C, the centripetal force is provided by tension in the wires holding the seats. Other types of force that can make objects move in circular paths include friction and gravity.

centripetal force

D The centripetal force here is supplied by friction between the tyres and the road.

 4 A satellite is in a circular orbit around the Earth. Explain how and why its velocity is continuously changing.

Exam-style question

Exam-style questions will follow on publication of the sample assessment materials by Edexcel.

Please see www.edexcel.com/gcsesci16 for more details.

Checkpoint

How confidently can you answer the questions at the top of the previous page?

Strengthen

S1 You are cycling along a flat road and your speed is increasing. Explain the resultant forces on you in the horizontal and vertical directions.

Extend

E1 Describe the forces on a human cannonball, from just before they are fired to when they land safely in a net, including how these forces affect their motion. You only need to consider forces and motion in the vertical direction.

E2 H Explain what a centripetal force is and describe three different kinds of force that can act as centripetal forces.

CP2c Mass and weight

Specification reference: P1.14

Progression questions

- What is the difference between mass and weight?
- What are the factors that determine the weight of an object?
- How do you calculate weight?

A The Huygens space probe used the air resistance from a parachute to balance its weight when it landed on Titan (one of Saturn's moons).

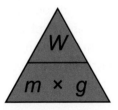

B This triangle can help you to change the subject of the formula. Cover up the quantity you want to find, and what you can see is the formula you need to use.

Did you know?

Gravity is not the same everywhere on the Earth. Your weight is greater standing at the North Pole than it would be standing at the equator.

Mass is the quantity of matter there is in an object, and only changes if the object itself changes. For example, your mass increases when you eat a meal. **Weight** is a measure of the pull of gravity on an object and depends on the strength of gravity. The units for mass are kilograms. Weight is a force, so it is measured in newtons.

 1 Suggest one way in which you can decrease your mass.

On Earth the **gravitational field strength** has a value of about 10 newtons per kilogram (N/kg). This means that each kilogram is pulled down with a force of 10 N. The gravitational field strength is different on other planets and moons.

The weight of an object can be calculated using the following formula:

$$\text{weight} = \text{mass} \times \text{gravitational field strength}$$
$$\text{(N)} \qquad \text{(kg)} \qquad \text{(N/kg)}$$

This is often written as: $W = m \times g$

Worked examples

What is the weight of a 90 kg astronaut on the surface of the Earth?

$W = m \times g$

$W = 90 \text{ kg} \times 10 \text{ N/kg}$

$= 900 \text{ N}$

A space probe has a weight of 3000 N on the Earth. What is its mass?

$m = \dfrac{W}{g}$

$= \dfrac{3000 \text{ N}}{10 \text{ N/kg}}$

$= 300 \text{ kg}$

2 A 300 kg space probe lands on Titan, where the gravitational field strength is 1.4 N/kg.

 a What is its mass on Titan? Explain your answer.

 b What is its weight on Titan?

 3 A Mars rover has a mass of 185 kg. Its weight on Mars is 685 N. What is the gravitational field strength on Mars?

Forces on falling bodies

On Earth, a falling object has a force of air resistance on it as well as its weight. Figure C shows how the forces on a skydiver change during her fall.

0.5 seconds after jumping, speed = 5 m/s

resultant

Air resistance increases with speed, so just after jumping the air resistance is much smaller than her weight. The large resultant force makes her accelerate downwards.

3 seconds after jumping, speed = 25 m/s

resultant

Her air resistance is larger but her weight stays the same. The resultant force is smaller, so she is still accelerating, but not as much.

12 seconds after jumping, speed = 55 m/s

resultant = 0

She is moving so fast that the air resistance balances her weight. She continues to fall at the same speed.

C

 4 Explain why the weight of the skydiver stays the same throughout the jump.

 5 When the skydiver opens her parachute her air resistance increases very suddenly. Explain how this affects the resultant force and her velocity.

Exam-style question

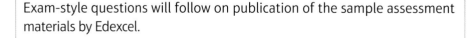

Exam-style questions will follow on publication of the sample assessment materials by Edexcel.

Please see www.edexcel.com/gcsesci16 for more details.

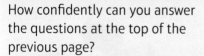
Checkpoint

How confidently can you answer the questions at the top of the previous page?

Strengthen

S1 Write glossary entries for 'mass' and 'weight'.

S2 A cat has a mass of 2 kg. Calculate its weight on Earth.

Extend

E1 Write an encyclopaedia entry that explains the difference between mass and weight.

E2 A space probe on Titan has a weight of 280 N. Calculate its mass and its weight on Earth.

CP2d Newton's Second Law

Specification reference: P1.13; P1.18

Progression questions

- What are the factors that affect the acceleration of an object?
- How do you calculate the different factors that affect acceleration?
- **H** What is inertial mass and how is it defined?

A The safety rules for building Formula 1® cars include a limit to the engine force and a minimum mass for the car.

The acceleration of an object is a measure of how much its velocity changes in a certain time. Sir Isaac Newton's Second Law of Motion describes the factors that affect the acceleration of an object.

The acceleration in the direction of a resultant force depends on:

- the size of the force (for the same mass, the bigger the force the bigger the acceleration)
- the mass of the object (for the same force, the more massive the object the smaller the acceleration).

Did you know?

B A bike with low mass is so important for track racers that their bikes do not even have brakes! Racing rules state that these bikes must have a minimum mass of 6.8 kg.

1 The resultant force on a ball is not zero. What will happen to the ball?

2 a The same force is used to accelerate a small car and a lorry. What will be different about their motions? Explain your answer.

b If you wanted to make the same two vehicles accelerate at the same rate, what can you say about the forces needed to do this? Explain your answer.

Calculating forces

The force needed to accelerate a particular object can be calculated using the formula:

force = mass × acceleration
  (N)   (kg)   (m/s^2)

This is often written as $F = m \times a$

1 newton is the force needed to accelerate a mass of 1 kg by 1 m/s^2.

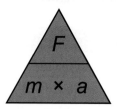

C This triangle can help you to change the subject of the formula. Cover up the quantity you want to find, and what you can see is the formula you need to use.

Worked example

A motorcycle has a mass of 200 kg. What force is needed to give it an acceleration of 7 m/s^2?

$F = m \times a$
= 200 kg × 7 m/s^2
= 1400 N

 3 A car has a mass of 1500 kg. What force is needed to give it an acceleration of 4 m/s^2?

 4 A force of 800 N accelerates the car in question 3. What is its acceleration?

D What do you need to know to work out whether the car or aeroplane has the greater acceleration?

H Inertial mass

The more massive an object is, the more force is needed to change its velocity (either to make it start moving or to change the velocity of a moving object). We define the **inertial mass** of an object as the force on it divided by the acceleration that force produces.

Calculating an object's inertial mass from values of force and acceleration gives the same mass value as that found by measuring the force of gravity on it.

 5 A force of 160 N on a bicycle produces an acceleration of 2 m/s^2. What is the total inertial mass of the bicycle and its rider?

Exam-style question

Exam-style questions will follow on publication of the sample assessment materials by Edexcel.

Please see www.edexcel.com/gcsesci16 for more details.

Checkpoint

How confidently can you answer the questions at the top of the previous page?

Strengthen

S1 Look at photo A. Explain whether the Formula 1® rules are designed to set an upper or lower limit to the accelerations of the cars.

S2 Calculate the force needed to accelerate a 250 kg motorbike at 5 m/s^2.

Extend

E1 Look at photo D. Explain what you need to know to help you to work out which vehicle will have the greater acceleration.

E2 Explain why two objects dropped on the Moon will accelerate at the same rate, even when they have different masses.

CP2e Newton's Third Law

Specification reference: P1.19

Progression questions

- What does Newton's Third Law tell us?
- How does Newton's Third Law apply to stationary objects?
- How do objects affect each other when they collide?

A The dog is not moving. What are the forces acting here?

B The Earth attracts the Moon with the same force as the Moon attracts the Earth.

2 You are standing leaning on a wall. Draw a sketch to show this (a stick man will do) and add arrows to show an action–reaction pair of forces acting in the:

a vertical direction

b horizontal direction.

3 For the situation in question 2, describe the balanced forces on you acting in the vertical direction.

Newton's Third Law is about the forces on two different objects when they interact with each other. This interaction can happen:

- when objects touch, such as when you sit on a chair
- at a distance, such as the gravitational attraction between the Earth and the Moon.

There is a pair of forces acting on the two interactive objects, often called **action–reaction forces**. The two forces are always the same size and in opposite directions. They are also the same type of force. In photo A the rope and the dog are both exerting pulling forces on each other. In photo B the two forces are both gravitational forces.

Photo A shows an **equilibrium** situation, because nothing is moving. A force in the rope is pulling on the dog but the dog is also pulling on the rope.

1 Think about the vertical forces in photo A. One force is the weight of the dog pushing down on the ground. What is the other force in this pair?

The weight of a dog on the ground is equal to the force pushing up on the dog from the ground. In photo A there is another pair of action–reaction forces acting on the rope and the dog – there is a force from the dog on the rope and a force from the rope on the dog.

Action–reaction forces are not the same as balanced forces. In both cases the sizes of the forces are equal and act in opposite directions, but:

- action–reaction forces act *on different objects*.
- balanced forces all act *on the same object*

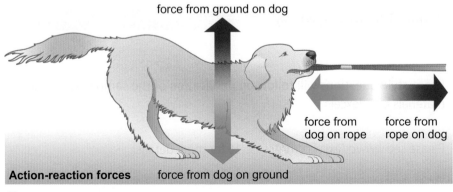

Action-reaction forces

Ci

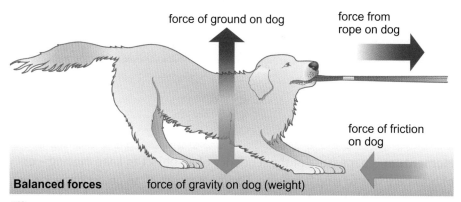

force of ground on dog

force from rope on dog

force of friction on dog

Balanced forces   force of gravity on dog (weight)

Cii

H Collisions

We can apply the idea of action–reaction forces to what happens when things collide. In photo D, the ball will bounce off the footballer's head. His head exerts a force on the ball, but the ball also exerts a force on his head, as you can feel if you have ever tried heading a ball!

The action and reaction forces that occur during the collision are the same size, but they do not necessarily have the same effects on the two objects, because the objects have different masses.

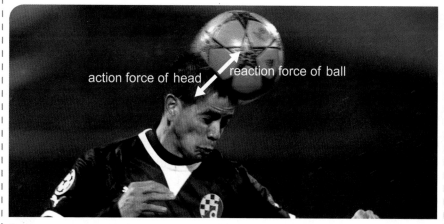

action force of head   reaction force of ball

D Action–reaction forces during a collision.

 4 Describe the action–reaction forces when a ball bounces on the ground.

 5 Look at photo D. The player's head and the ball both change velocity during the collision. Describe the effects on the two objects and explain why the effects are different.

Exam-style question

Exam-style questions will follow on publication of the sample assessment materials by Edexcel.

Please see www.edexcel.com/gcsesci16 for more details.

Checkpoint

How confidently can you answer the questions at the top of the previous page?

Strengthen

S1 Describe the action–reaction forces when you sit in a chair. Describe how these forces are different to a pair of balanced forces acting on you.

Extend

E1 Two teams are having a tug-of-war. Make a sketch and add labelled arrows to show three action–reaction force pairs and three pairs of balanced forces.

E2 **H** A ball is released a metre above the surface of the Earth. Describe the action–reaction forces due to gravity on the ball and the Earth. Describe the forces when the ball and the Earth collide. Explain how the effects on the two objects are different.

CP2f Momentum

Specification reference: P1.19; P1.20; P1.21

Progression questions

- How is momentum calculated?
- How is momentum related to force and acceleration?
- What happens to momentum in collisions?

A The damage caused by a wrecking ball depends on its mass and how fast it is moving when it hits.

force, mass and acceleration	$F = m \times a$
change in velocity and time	$a = \dfrac{v - u}{t}$

C formulae involving acceleration

Did you know?

The largest ships are oil tankers. It can take several miles for a moving oil tanker to come to a stop.

 4 A 1000 kg car accelerates from rest to 15 m/s in 15 seconds. What resultant force caused this?

Momentum is a measure of the tendency of an object to keep moving – or of how hard it is to stop it moving. The momentum of an object depends on its mass and its velocity. Momentum depends on a vector quantity (velocity), and is also a vector.

Momentum is calculated using this formula:

momentum = mass × velocity
  (kg m/s)   (kg)   (m/s)

This can also be written as $p = m \times v$, where p stands for momentum.

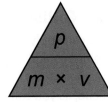

B

1 Explain why a motorcycle travelling at 30 m/s has less momentum than a car travelling at the same velocity.

2 A 500 kg wrecking ball is moving at 10 m/s when it hits a building. What is its momentum?

3 The same ball at a different time has a momentum of 1500 kg m/s. What is its velocity?

Momentum and acceleration

Table C shows two formulae involving acceleration. These can be combined to give:

$$\text{force} = \frac{\text{mass} \times \text{change in velocity}}{\text{time}} \quad \text{or} \quad \frac{m(v - u)}{t}$$

where v is the final velocity and u is the starting velocity.

As mass × velocity is the momentum of an object, this formula can also be written as:

$$\text{force} = \frac{\text{change in momentum}}{\text{time}} \quad \text{or} \quad \frac{mv - mu}{t}$$

Worked example

A 2000 kg car accelerates from 10 m/s to 25 m/s in 10 seconds. What resultant force produced this acceleration?

$$\text{force} = \frac{mv - mu}{t}$$

$$= \frac{2000 \text{ kg} \times 25 \text{ m/s} - 2000 \text{ kg} \times 10 \text{ m/s}}{10 \text{ s}}$$

$$= \frac{50\,000 \text{ kg m/s} - 20\,000 \text{ kg m/s}}{10 \text{ s}}$$

$$= 3000 \text{ N}$$

H Momentum and collisions

When moving objects collide the total momentum of both objects is the same before the collision as it is after the collision, as long as there are no external forces acting. This is known as **conservation of momentum**. Remember, momentum is a vector so you need to consider direction when you add the quantities together. If two objects are moving in opposite directions, we give the momentum of one object a positive sign and the other a negative sign.

$m =$ 20 kg	$m =$ 20 kg
$v =$ 6 m/s	$v =$ 0 m/s

before collision

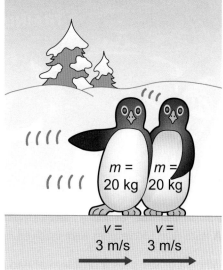

$m =$ 20 kg	$m =$ 20 kg
$v =$ 3 m/s	$v =$ 3 m/s

after collision

E

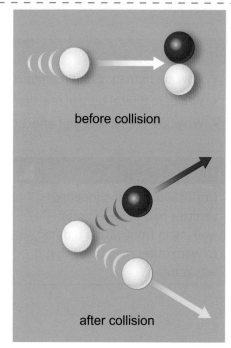

before collision

after collision

D The total momentum of the two coloured balls will be the same as the momentum of the white ball that hit them.

5 Look at diagram E.

 a Calculate the momentum of each penguin before they collide.

 b Calculate the total momentum before the penguins collide.

 c In which direction is the total momentum before the collision?

 d What is the total momentum after the collision and in which direction?

 e Explain whether momentum has been conserved.

Exam-style question

Exam-style questions will follow on publication of the sample assessment materials by Edexcel.

Please see www.edexcel.com/gcsesci16 for more details.

Checkpoint

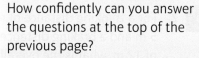

How confidently can you answer the questions at the top of the previous page?

Strengthen

S1 Two 5000 kg railway trucks are travelling at 5 m/s in opposite directions when they collide. After the collision they are stationary. Show that momentum is conserved.

Extend

E1 A 1 g bullet is travelling at 300 m/s when it enters a stationary 1 kg block of wood. The impact of the bullet makes the wood move. What is the speed of the block immediately after the impact? Explain how you worked out your answer.

CP2g Stopping distances

Specification reference: P1.22; P1.23; P1.24

Progression questions

- How are human reaction times measured?
- What are typical human reaction times?
- What are the factors that affect the stopping distance of a vehicle?

Did you know?

Until 1896 all 'self-propelled' vehicles had to have a man walking in front with a red flag, to warn other road users that it was coming.

A More than 130 vehicles were involved in this crash and over 200 people were injured.

1 Why is it important for drivers to know their stopping distances?

2 For a thinking distance of 5 m and a braking distance of 12 m, what is the overall stopping distance?

When a driver sees a problem ahead, their vehicle will travel some distance while the driver reacts to the situation. This is called the **thinking distance**. The vehicle will then go some distance further while the brakes are working to bring it to a halt. This is called the **braking distance**. The overall **stopping distance** for any road vehicle is the sum of the thinking and braking distances.

stopping distance = thinking distance + braking distance

Reaction times

A **reaction time** is the time between a person detecting a **stimulus** (such as a flashing light or a sound) and their **response** (such as pressing a button or applying the brakes in a car). Response times can be measured using computers or electric circuits that measure the time between a stimulus and a response.

The typical reaction time to a visual stimulus, such as a computer screen changing colour, is about 0.25 seconds. However this time can be much longer if the person is tired, ill or has been taking drugs or drinking alcohol. Distractions, such as using a mobile phone, can also increase reaction times.

3 Explain why the thinking distance depends on:

   a the driver's reaction time   **b** the speed of the car.

4 Suggest why the reaction time measured in a driving simulator might be longer than the time measured using a test on a computer.

5 Explain why there are legal limits for the amount of alcohol drivers are allowed in their blood.

B A driving simulator can be used to test reaction times in a realistic situation.

Braking distances

Car brakes use friction to slow the car down. If the brakes are worn, they create less friction and do not slow the vehicle as effectively. Friction between the tyres and road is also important. If the road is wet or has loose gravel on it, or if the tyres are worn, there is less friction and the braking distance is increased.

If a vehicle has more mass, more force is needed to decelerate it. So if the same amount of friction is used to stop a vehicle, a heavier vehicle will travel further than a lighter one (it has a greater braking distance).

 6 Why are the overall stopping distances for cars less than for lorries?

 7 Look at photo D. Suggest why there are two separate speed limits.

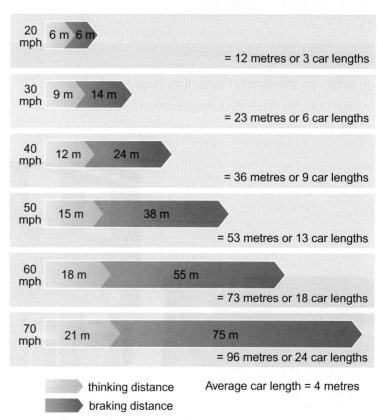

20 mph	6 m	6 m		= 12 metres or 3 car lengths
30 mph	9 m	14 m		= 23 metres or 6 car lengths
40 mph	12 m	24 m		= 36 metres or 9 car lengths
50 mph	15 m	38 m		= 53 metres or 13 car lengths
60 mph	18 m	55 m		= 73 metres or 18 car lengths
70 mph	21 m	75 m		= 96 metres or 24 car lengths

thinking distance

braking distance

Average car length = 4 metres

C The Highway Code shows typical stopping distances for a family car.

D This sign is from an autoroute (motorway) in France. The speed limits are in km/h.

Exam-style question

Exam-style questions will follow on publication of the sample assessment materials by Edexcel.

Please see www.edexcel.com/gcsesci16 for more details.

Checkpoint

How confidently can you answer the questions at the top of the previous page?

Strengthen

S1 List the factors that affect stopping distance. State whether each factor affects the thinking distance or the braking distance, and how they affect this distance.

Extend

E1 The crash in photo A happened in a sudden patch of fog. Write a paragraph for a road-safety website to explain why fog can be a hazard on the roads, and what drivers can do to avoid crashing in foggy conditions.

CP2h Crash hazards

Specification reference: P1.26

Progression questions

- What are the dangers caused by large decelerations?
- How can the hazards of large decelerations be reduced?
- **H** How can you use momentum to calculate the forces involved in crashes?

A The amount of damage caused by a collision depends on the mass of the lorry and on how fast it was travelling.

B The large forces in road collisions injure or kill people and damage cars.

C Forces on humans can result from hitting the dashboard or steering wheel, or if other passengers hit them.

In a car crash, the vehicles involved come to a stop very quickly. Slowing down is a **deceleration** (or a negative acceleration). The force needed for any kind of acceleration depends on the size of the acceleration and on the mass of the object.

1 Explain why the force on a vehicle in a crash is larger:

a if the vehicle is moving faster before the crash

b for a lorry than for a car travelling at the same speed.

Modern cars have lots of safety features built into them to help to reduce the forces on the occupants in a collision. **Crumple zones** are built into the front (and sometimes the back) of cars. If the car hits something it takes a little time for this crumpling to happen, so the deceleration of the car is less and the force on the car is also less than if it had a more solid front.

Photo C also shows that the passengers do not stop moving when the car stops! Seat belts hold the passengers into the car, so the effect of the crumple zone reduces the forces on the passengers as well as on the car. Airbags increase the time it takes for a person's head to stop in a collision.

D Airbags were used to help the Mars Pathfinder to land safely by increasing the time for the probe to hit the ground, and so reducing the force on it..

 2 Look at photo C. Explain why front *and* back seat passengers in a car should wear seat belts.

 3 Bubble wrap is a plastic covering with many air bubbles. How do you think bubble wrap protects fragile items?

H

The force in a road collision depends on the change of momentum as the car comes to a stop. You have seen (in Topic CP2f Momentum) that we can use the formula below to calculate the force:

$F = \dfrac{mv - mu}{t}$, where u is initial velocity and v is final velocity.

Worked example

A 1500 kg car is travelling at 15 m/s (just over 30 mph) when it hits a wall. It comes to a stop in 0.07 seconds. What is the force acting on the car?

$$\text{force} = \frac{1500 \text{ kg} \times 0 \text{ m/s} - 1500 \text{ kg} \times 15 \text{ m/s}}{0.07 \text{ s}}$$

$$= \frac{-22\,500}{0.07}$$

$$= -321\,429 \text{ N}$$

The negative sign shows that the force is in the opposite direction to the original motion.

 4 a **H** An 1800 kg car travelling at 20 m/s stops in 0.03 seconds when it hits a wall. What is the force on it?

 b **H** Explain why this force is different to the one in the worked example. Give as many reasons as you can.

Did you know?

Many people have survived falls from aeroplanes without parachutes. In 2004, skydiver Christine McKenzie's parachute failed – she escaped with only a cracked pelvis because she fell into some power lines which slowed her down before she hit the ground.

Checkpoint

How confidently can you answer the questions at the top of the previous page?

Strengthen

S1 Describe two ways of reducing the forces in a collision, and explain how they work.

Extend

E1 **H** Use calculations to show the effects of velocity, mass and crumple zones on the forces acting in a road collision. You will need to find or estimate values for speed, mass and the change in length of a crumple zone in a crash.

Exam-style question

Exam-style questions will follow on publication of the sample assessment materials by Edexcel.

Please see www.edexcel.com/gcsesci16 for more details.

Term 1

Exam-style questions and sample student answers with expert commentary and exam tips will follow on publication of the sample assessment materials by Edexcel.

Please see www.edexcel.com/gcsesci16 for more details.